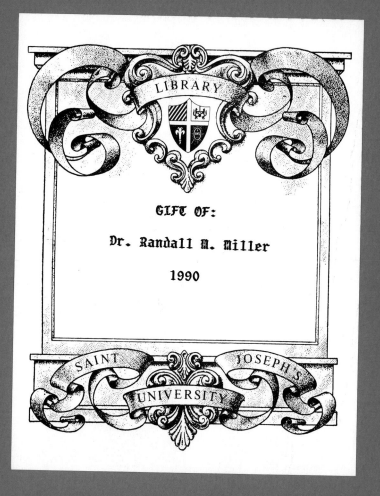

AMERICANA LIBRARY

ROBERT E. BURKE, EDITOR

THE CASUAL LABORER
AND OTHER ESSAYS

BY
CARLETON H. PARKER

Introduction to the Original Edition
by Cornelia Stratton Parker

Introduction to the Americana Library Edition
by Harold M. Hyman

UNIVERSITY OF WASHINGTON PRESS
SEATTLE AND LONDON

Library of Congress Cataloging in Publication Data
Parker, Carleton Hubbell, 1879-1918.
    The casual laborer, and other essays.
    (Americana library, AL-25)
    CONTENTS: Toward understanding labor unrest.—The
casual laborer.—The I.W.W.—Motives in economic life.
    Includes bibliographical references.
    1. Labor and laboring classes—U.S. 2. Industrial
Workers of the World. I. Title.
HD8072.P25   1972   331'.0973   76-172904
ISBN 0-295-95184-2

TO
THORSTEIN VEBLEN

CONTENTS

INTRODUCTION
TO THE 1972 EDITION

"PROFESSOR Parker's work was so important that the general public ought to know what it was," a *New York Times* book reviewer concluded in mid-1920, soon after Carleton H. Parker's *The Casual Laborer and Other Essays* appeared in print.[1] The *Times* writer expressed a contemporary consensus. Other serious journalists, contributors to reformist Progressive periodicals, and learned-journal reviewers of Parker's *Casual Laborer* appreciated his insights into the causes and remedies

1. *The New York Times*, 20 June 1920. Parker's *The Casual Laborer and Other Essays* (New York: Harcourt, Brace, and Howe, 1920) contained an introduction by his widow, Mrs. Cornelia Stratton Parker. Hereafter I cite this volume as *Casual Laborer*, in order to distinguish it from Mrs. Parker's *An American Idyll: The Life of Carleton H. Parker* (Boston: Atlantic Monthly Press, 1919), which I cite hereafter as *American Idyll*. Documentation in monographs cited in these footnotes contains such full references to relevant primary and secondary sources that I decided against repeating them. Instead, I thank the authors involved for their diligent mining of archives, libraries, and other information depositories.

of labor unrest, particularly among migrant workers. Approving comment centered especially on Parker's views about the "Wobblies" (members of the Industrial Workers of the World), "casual"—that is, itinerant—workers who had developed since the century's turn a revolutionary rhetoric worrisome even to self-professed friends of organized labor. Parker's *Casual Laborer* was also reviewed in publications normally closed to the theorizings of academic authors, in part because in 1920 the nation was experiencing a "red scare," marked by antipathy to all organized labor. Interest in the Wobblies was high, if not always critical.[2]

The Casual Laborer deserved, and received, relatively large attention for a better reason than ascendant antiradicalism, however. Professor Parker had had the opportunity—rare for an academic scholar—to use his ideas and theories as the base for actual, significant policy and imaginative institutionalizing. Dur-

2. Robert Murray, *Red Scare: A Study in National Hysteria, 1919-1920* (Minneapolis: University of Minnesota Press, 1955); Melvyn Dubofsky, *We Shall Be All: A History of the Industrial Workers of the World* (Chicago: Quadrangle, 1969): Irving Bernstein, *The Lean Years: A History of the American Worker, 1920-1933* (Boston: Houghton Mifflin Company, 1960), chaps. i-iv.

ing the period of United States participation in the World War (April 1917–November 1918), Parker had placed himself and his scholarly judgments about migrant workers and the IWW in the nation's service. To his "civilian" duties as dean of the University of Washington's College of Business Administration and head of that university's Department of Economics, Parker added an astonishing miscellany of war-related activities. Within weeks of the war declaration, he had become adviser on labor matters to Washington's governor, labor counselor to the state's Council of National Defense, and an overworked, unresting field agent for many federal and state mediation, conciliation, and raw materials production agencies.[3]

Responsibilities imposed by these manifold commitments brought Parker into contact with the explosive labor-management situation, left over from prewar decades, that plagued the west coast lumber industry. Drawing upon his unique scholarship (which would be published in 1920 in *The Casual Laborer*), Parker played a primary role in transforming what appeared

3. Parker, *American Idyll,* pp. 136-78.

to be imminent disaster into a constructive pioneering experiment in applied social science. *The Casual Laborer* deserved respectful review attention in 1920 because its underlying theories and attitudes were not mere professional pondering, but were the basis for practical solutions that had worked in 1917-18. After Parker's innovative suggestions were institutionalized in the fall of 1917, the great majority of the Pacific Northwest's Wobblies abstained from the anticipated industrial sabotage, strikes, slowdowns, and anticapitalist pacifist propaganda; refrained even from wandering casually from job to job. As a result, Pacific Northwest forests provided more material than fabricators could devour for war planes, ships, and barracks. Reviewers of *The Casual Laborer* concurred that Parker had helped to win an important home-front campaign. And they knew the costs to himself, to his family, and to future scholarship.

Utterly overworked in the nation's service, Parker became a victim of the wartime influenza epidemic. He died in the spring of 1918, only forty years old. But before his final collapse he had achieved major successes. Parker convinced the militantly antiwar Wobblies to associate with the United States Army. Exploiting academic acquaintanceships with such Progressive leaders as Felix Frankfurter and Walter Lippmann, among others, and with University of Washington President Henry Suzzallo and California Institute of Technology[4] President J. A. B. Scherer, who represented the Council of National Defense, Parker inspired the army to sponsor creation of a labor union whose rank-and-file were civilian "timber stiffs"—Wobblies in the main—and whose officials were uniformed military officers! Still further, Parker pressured American Federation of Labor locals, long hostile to the Wobblies, into affiliation with his hybrid "union." Lumber barons (heretofore irreconcilably anti-any-union), county sheriffs, city police chiefs, and county, state, and federal attorneys (long the spearheads of local anti-Wobbly activism) added to the motley elements of Parker's creation. The upshot was vast lumber production. It was achieved without bloodshed, vigilantism, or harsh repression. There were absolute improvements in

4. Known then as Throop Institute.

living and working conditions for the industry's long-abused workers, and in worker participation in certain decision-making procedures. Most of the physical improvements, at least, outlasted the war. The Parker organization provided even Wobbly workmen with physical and psychological stakes in companies and communities, and substantially decreased the traditionally peripatetic characteristic of many timber stiffs.

Fifty years ago, reviewers of *The Casual Laborer* stressed the point that Parker had succeeded as fast and as far as he did because, almost unique among Americans in 1917, he had been prepared through the precedent scholarship represented in *The Casual Laborer* (which, though published in 1920, contained his prewar research and judgments) to search rationally for alternatives to repression with respect to Wobbly migrant workers. He became a member of a group still small in World War I—a policy-making professor.[5]

5. *The New Republic,* 26 May 1920, pp. 424-25; Virgil Jordan in *The Dial* 69 (1920):96-101; Florence Richardson in *Journal of Political Economy* 28 (1920):622-24; W. L. Chaney in *The Survey,* 2 October 1920, p. 26; H. A. Overstreet in *The Nation* 3 (1920):455; Harold M. Hyman, *Soldiers and Spruce: The Origins and Purposes of the Army's Labor Union*

Parker's multiple wartime titles, hurtling pace, and large successes must not conceal the fact that his was the pioneer's lonely role, lonely in ways difficult to appreciate today. In the 1970s major labor strife of the sort Parker frustrated triggers into action echelons of ready institutions and cadres of responsible, trained men. Unions are respectable, management is reasonable, and agencies of government on every level of the federal system are resourceful. Mediation, conciliation, and arbitration procedures are well-developed. Courts and law have dropped antilabor traditions. Today's universities sustain sophisticated industrial relations institutes and economics, political science, and sociology professors, who study labor conditions with clinical skill. There are enormous resources of amassed data and monographic research. Supplemental funds from private foundations aid off- and on-campus efforts to meliorate labor-management clashes.

---

of World War I, The Loyal Legion of Loggers and Lumbermen (Berkeley and Los Angeles: University of California Press, 1963), pp. 50-104; Robert L. Tyler, *Rebels of the Woods: The I.W.W. in the Pacific Northwest* (Eugene: University of Oregon Books, 1967), chap. iv.

In 1917 none of these things existed, although for a decade or more Progressive pedagogues of Parker's sort had stressed the need for systematic applications of universities' talents and of government resources in the solutions of pressing labor problems. In these senses as in others, the United States went to war haphazardly indeed. The spring of national government—M. I. Ostrogorski's phrase —was so weak as to drive some responsible officials to desperate innovations.[6]

The absence in April 1917 of enough government institutions, informed experts, or useful programs compounded the odds against anyone coping rationally with the problems in the Northwest. Timber operators refused to

6. G. C. Reinhardt and W. R. Kintner, *The Haphazard Years: How America Has Gone to War* (Garden City, N.Y.: Doubleday, 1960), pp. 15-117; M. I. Ostrogorski, *Democracy and the Organization of Political Parties* (London, 1902), 2:550-99, esp. p. 577, and *passim*. American industry may have "come of age," as E. C. Kirkland suggests, sometime between Appomattox and the century's turn. But the facts of 1917 suggest that business, labor, and public policy were far from mature interrelationships. Edward Chase Kirkland, *Industry Comes of Age: Business, Labor and Public Policy, 1860-1897* (New York: Holt, Rinehart and Winston, 1961), p. 127 and *passim;* Robert D. Cuff, "Woodrow Wilson and Business-Government Relations during World War I," *Journal of Politics* 31 (1969): 385-407.

listen to complaints of itinerant timber workers, who protested, sometimes through sabotage, against outrageous deficiencies in living, eating, and working conditions. For their part, Wobblies responded with radical, pacifist rhetoric and threatened to impede production by means of strikes and walkouts, if not worse. Until Parker won a trial for his views, law-and-order advocates initiated vigilante actions as well as court prosecutions against IWW members. Even when legal procedures held firm, IWW card-holders faced hostile police and judges. "Respectable" labor unions such as those in the AFL, themselves weak in contests against unsympathetic employers and hostile legal traditions, scorned common cause with the IWW.

Considering these harsh attitudes, the magnitude of Parker's accomplishments looms larger. This innovative student of prewar migrant workers transformed pioneering scholarship into inspirations for intellectuals-at-war, including John Dewey, Felix Frankfurter, and Walter Lippmann, military professionals including John J. Pershing, prominent timber barons, and thousands of nameless woodsmen. His career, which his widow described as an American idyll, deserves retelling.[7]

Carleton H. Parker was born into a farming family of Vacaville, California, on 31 March 1878. Eighteen years later, he was a freshman engineering student of the University of California. Uncertain about goals, Parker dropped out of college to try newspaper reporting in Idaho and Spokane, but family pressure returned him to Berkeley. There, as an overaged senior in the fall of 1903, he met Cornelia Stratton, and a romance flourished quickly. Perhaps to prevent it from advancing toward marriage, Parker's family sent him on a trip abroad. In South Africa, the fledgling mining engineer encountered unsavory repressive labor-control techniques. After returning to Berkeley, for several months in 1906 Parker served as a lecturer in the university's new Extension Division, then initiating its adventure in continuing education.

When Parker and Miss Stratton decided to marry, he adopted a new, presumably more re-

7. Hyman, *Soldiers and Spruce,* pp. 53-96 and *passim;* Tyler, *Rebels of the Woods,* chap. iv.

munerative, career as a bond salesman. But the wedding was 7 September 1907, just when a severe financial depression was discouraging investors. Parker's discontent with "securities" was increased further by his taste of teaching and academic research, and the fact that his interests had shifted toward labor economics. Therefore, the young father, nearing his thirtieth birthday and boasting slim financial resources, moved his little family to Harvard. Later, with wife and two babies in tow, Parker settled in Heidelberg, and then Munich, so that he could work toward a doctorate in economics at the University of Heidelberg. A University of California instructorship followed his *summa cum laude* dissertation on "The Labor Policy of the American Trust." But trouble waited at Berkeley.

Taking temporary leave from teaching duties, in 1914 Parker accepted appointment as executive secretary of California's new Immigration and Housing Commission. Powerful commercial and university interests were offended by his efforts to raise standards in some migrant labor camps. His offensiveness increased sharply with publication of his report on the Wheatland Hop Fields' Riot of 3 August 1913, during which four men were killed when a sheriff's posse tried to break strikers' picket lines. Parker's report was a scholarly condemnation of the law's prejudiced agents and of the psychological and environmental conditions that drove the migrant workmen to strike and to violence. Such heresies resulted in Parker's resigning (October 1914) from the California commission.[8]

Having returned again (January 1915) to Berkeley, Parker studied Freud while he taught labor problems. But increasingly strained Berkeley campus relationships prompted Parker to accept the invitation from the University of Washington's ambitious new president, Henry Suzzallo, to be head of the Department of Economics and dean of the College of Business Administration.

Soon after, the United States entered the war. Almost at once Parker began to serve the hastily created Cantonments Adjustments Commission of the Council of National De-

8. Carleton H. Parker, "The California Casual and His Revolt," *Quarterly Journal of Economics* (1915); reprinted in *The Casual Laborer,* pp. 61-89, as "The Casual Laborer." Biographical details are in Parker, *American Idyll,* pp. 1-90.

fense, mediating grievances expressed by skilled workmen building the huge training base near Tacoma, Camp Lewis. Simultaneously strikes were spreading throughout the lumber industry. From timber supply to lumber use, the nation's war work was being curtailed. Parker rejected angry suggestions from lumber operators that the industry's restless unskilled workers were pro-German traitors or dedicated anticapitalist revolutionaries best put down by police or even by doughboys (an eventuality dreaded by the army, which wanted every man possible mustered into the AEF to serve abroad). "It is a strike to better conditions," Parker informed his wife. "The I.W.W. are only the display feature. The main body of opinion is from a lot of unskilled workers who are sick of the filthy bunk-houses and rotten grub."[9] Snatching time from university responsibilities and mediation meetings, Parker tried to check excess on all sides. Meanwhile, he worked through Frankfurter and Lippmann, who were special assistants to the secretary of war and the attorney general, as well as Suzzallo and Scherer, who were hyperactive

9. Parker, *American Idyll,* p. 136.

in high-level home-front war work, to disseminate his environmental ideas about the true causes and possible cures of the casual laborer's unrest in the Northwest. Because Parker's conclusions concerning the reasons why men joined the IWW meshed with the nation's need for unconstrained production of Northwest timber, he managed to harmonize class-consciousness, self-interest, and patriotism. Then he died.

Whether admiringly, as in Progressive journals of opinion, or resentfully, when certain lumbermen spoke of Parker's work, a heavy contemporary consensus depicted Parker as essentially sympathetic to the Wobblies, his special interest of long standing among migrant workers.[10] But when the first full-scale historical scholarship on the IWW appeared in 1969, Parker's purposes in his World War I work received an opposite interpretation. Parker was "hostile to the IWW," the author, Melvyn Dubofsky, concluded.[11]

10. See "The I.W.W.," in Parker, *Casual Laborer,* pp. 91-124, reprinted from *Atlantic Monthly* (November 1917). It was commissioned by the periodical's editor, Ellery Sedgwick, and reflected Carleton Parker's intense interest in the IWW going back a decade; note Mrs. Parker's comment in *Casual Laborer,* p. 7.
11. Dubofsky, *We Shall Be All,* p. 299.

Historians may never resolve satisfactorily the complexities and subtleties of motivation analysis. Still, the divergence between judgments in 1920 and 1970 about Parker's attitudes toward the Wobblies invites further inquiry. The best source of evidence on Parker —in the absence of new primary materials, such as his unpublished research results or personal letters, diaries, or journals—remains, and will remain, his *Casual Laborer*.[12]

The Casual Laborer deserves to be reissued and to receive new attention for larger reasons than this, however. The entire published research of an inadequately recognized pioneering scholar and Progressive policy-maker, *The Casual Laborer* is relevant to the 1970s. For today militant radicals absorb eclectically the revolutionary ideologies to which Wobblies of Woodrow Wilson's White House years responded, including Bakuninian anarchist preachments to "propaganda of the deed" and "direct action." Parker insisted that the rhetoric should not mislead; that environmental

12. On 5 October 1970 Mrs. Parker wrote me that about twenty years ago a fire destroyed all of Carleton Parker's unpublished scholarly and personal materials. The approach to subsequent research Parker would probably have followed had his death not intervened is suggested in Parker, *Casual Laborer*, pp. 14-19.

causes explained the Wobblies' sullen underground harassment of employers and of the society they found repressive.[13] In the insight that hindsight allows, *The Casual Laborer* stands forward as a major reason why in 1917-18 Wobbly assumptions about mainstream America did not come true; why potentialities for suppression and repression among wartime officialdom and citizenry remained unrealized. In the Quaker phrase, *The Casual Laborer* speaks to our concerns.

HAROLD M. HYMAN

Houston, Texas
November 1971

---

13. Dubofsky, *We Shall Be All*, pp. 147, 292.

THE CASUAL LABORER

INTRODUCTION

A TREMENDOUS responsibility rests upon anyone who undertakes to publish posthumous writings. Even though they may have been written to appear in print here and there, one cannot be sure that in later years the author would have wished them given to a wider public in more permanent form. Yet the time may come, as I feel it has in this case, when the value in publishing certain manuscripts seems greater than the drawback that possibly their author would have preferred to let them rest in more or less oblivion.

The only real reluctance I feel about publishing the following papers concerns itself with the first manuscript, and one which in many respects is perhaps the most vital paper of all. This article was not written for publication in any form. Back in the winter of 1916, Carl Parker journeyed East on what has been termed his Research Magnificent, to lay his thesis, mulled over until then in comparative solitude in his Berkeley hillside

3

study, before the big minds of the country in his field.

In New York, Boston, Philadelphia, Baltimore, his soul exulted in chance after chance for telling discussions and arguments concerning his loved subject, the application of the newer psychology to a study of labor problems. Letter after letter brought back to California accounts of rich conversations with the men he had most hoped to interest in his thesis, and the resultant stimulus and encouragement. Along toward Christmas he felt the time had come when he should put his thesis into writing and thereby receive even more definite criticism from the men whose ideas he valued. This he did, and under date of January 6th, 1917, he wrote: ". . . I redressed my talk down and raced to read it to Professor Hollingworth. We spent four hours on it and I had numerous criticisms and hints. None adverse to the thesis, only suggestions as to places where I might strengthen it. . . . I read my paper to Walter Lippmann tomorrow and then Monday I'll be ready to type it and get carbons to send you. All tomorrow morning I'll labor on getting it into better shape. *Of course it is written in part to call out comments, so the statements are strong and unmodified.* I am sure that I'll see just how it will be developed into a complete book form before I am done with this reading of it. I feel it in my bones. . . ." This paper I have titled: "Toward Understanding Labor Unrest." In a chronological arrangement it would have appeared second. It gives a perspective to Carl Parker's approach to the study of labor problems; it is the most intimate paper of all — it was given first place.

The second paper, "The Casual Laborer," appeared in 1915 in the November *Quarterly Journal of Economics* under the title "The California Casual and His Revolt." From November, 1913, to November, 1914, Carl Parker was Executive Secretary of the California State Immigration and Housing Commission. In the spring of 1914 he was deputized to investigate the Wheatland Hopfield Riot for the Federal Government. As intimated in the first paper, perhaps this was as fruitful an incident, judged from the intellectual viewpoint, as he ever experienced. By its very dramatic quality, it focused his interest, as it focused the interest of the State, on the problem of the migratory, the casual, the I. W. W. From that time on he kept pegging away at the whys and wherefores, and at the very time of his death was more intent than ever on understanding the lower strata of labor, their troubles and the possible solutions. Somehow the glaring inadequacy of even supposedly intellectual handling of the labor problem ate into his soul from the time of the investigation of that Riot on, and he gave up the rest of his life to digging as far below the surface of labor unrest as he could get.

In January, 1917, he addressed a gathering of Wharton School people in Philadelphia on the subject of the Western Labor Problem, and the Wheatland case in particular. I came across the following notes, the introduction to that talk:

"Any university, or in fact any modern, analysis of the labor problem is composed of a series of formal briefs on temporary instruments which for the moment find themselves used in industrial society, such as conciliation and arbitration, apprenticeship, trade union structure, child labor legislation. University labor treatment is a photographic sub-science. It is like a New Hampshire village church service to a decayed gentlewoman: it is sane and gently daring. It has the pleasant reactions of slumming in a picturesque but not underfed immigrant quarter. Labor, to the undergraduate, is an *interesting* subject.

"The real labor problem is not this. It is one of individual psychology. What are men when they die as laborers or business men? What kind of grandchildren follow them? What is their social heredity? What is the psychic balance sheet? It is a relation between a plastic, sensitive, easily degenerated nervous organism called "man" and an environment. The product is human character. The labor problem is one of character-formation. . . . The importance of the western labor problem is that a *human,* irrational, de-mechanized, dynamite-using labor type rose and functioned. . . ."

The third paper, on "The I. W. W.," is a reprint from the *Atlantic Monthly* of November 1917, written at the request of the Editor, Mr. Sedgwick. No one can claim that Carl Parker took a detached academic view of the I. W. W. without any actual contact with the class of whom it wrote. From the time of the Wheatland Hopfield Riot to his death, he was only at rare intervals ever out of touch with the I. W. W. movement, studying it first hand at every possible point. He numbered many personal friends and enemies among I. W. Ws. To him the problem was never one of three letters in large type on the front page of the morning paper. Human Beings made up the movement — not all of them awaited eagerly by Saint Peter at the Starry Gates, yet just as true not all doomed to boil forever in the caldrons of the damned. Not every Republican or Democrat is a chosen emissary of the Lord.

The reaction to this I. W. W. article interested us greatly. One business periodical of the Northwest grew almost breathless in alarm — the State University was harboring a dangerous rebel in its midst — he might even be a Socialist! The only safe thing was to do away with him. But on the whole, readers were extremely interested in Carl Parker's viewpoint. I have before me some of the letters that came in from friends and strangers and the carbons of his replies. These latter are more informal than scholarly in their mode of expression. One friend wrote from Canada: ". . . I want to thank you for the calmness with which you have discussed these people and for the way in which you have brought it home (at least to my way of thinking) to society that the I. W. W. is of its own spawning. Your insistence on the psychological analysis is most opportune. . . ."

In part the reply ran as follows: ". . . That article of mine which you referred to would more

or less tell you where my modern interests lie. I
have had a good deal better reports on it than I
thought I would. . . . I feel that the general
unrest is spreading so fast that this nippy little
civilization of ours will literally go to pot unless
we do something to iron out the economic and
psychological inequality. The riots in Germany
today are to the point. If we had a Napoleon
scheming it we couldn't have a more developed
unrest than there is in the Pacific Northwest. The
working classes, both skilled and unskilled, suspect the war and the Government, the aims of
the Allies, the aims of the Germans, and the aims
of the business men; and the business men and
the Allies and the Germans all suspect the working men. Both sides suspect the intellectuals and
the intellectuals are sore at both sides, and no-
body has gotten any relief and so on and so on.
The Department of Justice is going to make us
all patriotic if it has to arrest and convict us in
order to do so. So, generally, Bill, somehow things
seem to be unrestful."

One of the country's big psychopathologists
wrote: ". . . I am glad to see that you are
in the School of Business Administration for I
know that the psychopathological point of view

will be of great use therein. I have just read your
article on the I. W. W. in the current *Atlantic*
and have been recommending it to everybody.
. . . Hoping some day to achieve the euphoria of the hobo, I am . . ." In reply to
this letter Carl Parker wrote: ". . . I think it
is up to the two of us to actually do something
for the euphoria of the hobo as well as for several
other tough-working subdivisions of his psychological nature. He is certainly now wearing a
stack of crowns of thorns reaching twenty to
thirty feet in the air vertically.

"The I. W. W. is the best little object of compensatory activity for the unheroic to work their
compensating patriotism off on that has existed
in modern times. . . . This is a great time to
live in the world and have a little abnormal psychological literature at your elbow. . . . I have
taken up my third job for the War Department
and am now mediating on a threatened longshoremen strike. The longshoremen have got the
Bolsheviki looking like a rather dilapidated
Christian Endeavor Convention. In their last
little economic struggle out here they killed off
some twenty participants and their present plans
remind one of what is alleged to be the plans of

the Bulgarians upon the prospect of their invasion
into Servia. As I said before this is a good time
to muss around in economic affairs."

A lawyer wrote: "I have not yet written and
told you what I think of your *Atlantic* article. It
is ripping, and I do not see how you could have
done better with it. A bunch of us were at O——'s
place a few Sundays ago and went over it together. . . . I have heard that even —— has
spoken approvingly of the article which is a trib-
ute to both of you, for it is not so very long since
—— was encouraging the Fresno police to 'drown
out the rats in the jail.' I hear that conditions
are already improving in the lumber camps up
your way and that the eight-hour day is now becoming the rule, also that the camp conditions are
greatly improved and the lot of the migratory
worker in the lumber camps is beginning to show
distinct signs of betterment, and I take great
pleasure in recogniing that you have had your
hand in all of this. . . ." In reply to this letter
Carl Parker wrote: ". . . I am just now more
excited over the Bolsheviki and its children, the
German strikes, than anything else that has hap-
pened. I could not see how men who had cast
loose their intellectual moorings from all the old

inequality conditions would ever contemplate
going back home and putting themselves meekly
into the industrial mess. I have an idea that the
psychic basis of these revolts is a fear of a resumption of the old life. It seems fair to prophesy that
the old order is done though of course it must influence the character of the new order. Even if
there should be an apparent resumption of the old
affairs in form, this would not last long. Over
here at American Lake you can hear all kinds of
the most radical of talk and I feel that some kind
of a new deal is on the boards for the post-war
period.

"Here in Seattle I am running up against a
pretty reactionary group of employers, but even
among them I find people who have read that
small *Atlantic Monthly* article and are anxious to
talk about it. I have gotten some fifty letters
from all kinds and conditions of people about
it. . . .

"I am working hard on trying to get the lumbermen to willingly clean up their camps and hold
some kind of a sincere hand out to the workers,
and I think I see perhaps where it is beginning to
bear fruit. I put over what was apparently a
slightly premature acceptance of the eight-hour

day in the entire lumber industry of the Spokane district. The operators now show a slight tendency to back slide. I am working for three federal commissions now on different labor troubles and I am learning a heap and getting batted over the head with monotonous frequency. . . ."

And lastly I quote from the letter of a strange Professor: ". . . I think you have put one over in your article on the I. W. W. in the current *Atlantic*. More of the same sort of thing in similar places will help the cause of liberalism and democracy enormously. . . ." And here Carl Parker wrote: ". . . I feel that the 'cure' of the I. W. W. lies in the well-known modern method of educational practice and theory and that the achievement of such a social renovation is much easier than our hysterical fellow patriots believe. It comes down to that sad old comparison between the use of suppression in contrast with a system of wise social prevention. At times I feel that those who pretend to be working patriotically for unity are, in fact, the active agents of serious disunity in our nation. Many seem to forget that being a melting pot carries with it certain serious attributes. . . ."

I find some loose pages of manuscript among Carl Parker's papers which give in a short space his approach to the I. W. W. and certain forms of labor unrest: ". . . The labor turnover statistics in America are startling. The growing employee inefficiency is a subconsciously planned neglecting of the work. Union recognition, the closed shop, the sympathetic strike, are not pursued by the unionist because of any deep realization of the ethical or strategic significance of the issue, but because it is a means of expressing resentment at the stresses and strains of their position. This diverted energy becomes a relief activity, an activity tending, curiously, to reestablish the unionist's dignity in his own eyes. It is impossible for man to suffer economic and social humiliation without an important feeling of inferiority, of *minderwürtigkeit*. A common cure for this, it has been observed, is a resort to some enterprise in pugnacity. In modern translation this means a strike of more or less violence, a riot, or at least some conflict with the law. Relief has been found by dissociation from social rule and giving some liberty and dominance to the more primitive desires of the sub-conscious. A rabid Socialist, an I. W. W. (even today a pacifist), has dissociated himself more or less completely from the going norms of society. His subconscious is completely in the saddle. His fixed idea is a mental complex supported by a strong emotion and runs back for its explaining cause to a life of extreme stress or privation or a neurasthenic disposition. The I. W. W. are recruited from the most degraded and unnaturally living of America's labor groups. Their inherited instincts are in toto either offered no opportunity for functioning, or are harshly repressed. They are without home security, have no sex life except the abnormal, they are hunted and scorned by society; normal leadership, emulation, constructiveness, is unknown to them. And it is both psychically and physiologically a sound deduction that they will at all social costs seek some relief activity. The one prerequisite for a permanent acquisition of crop- and barnburning as a habit for this migratory group is that the law and society should show itself properly and openly fearful. This, as events in California, Arizona, and the Middle West show, is the very contribution of society. Deportation, bull-pens, imprisonment, is food for the sore dignity of the syndicalist. It is the psychological parallel to the newspaper publicity of the ego crazed murderer. . . ."

Also I came across the following short and to-the-point statement of what Carl Parker considered the I. W. W. problem: "The I. W. W. is a symptom of a distressing industrial status. For the moment the relation of its activities to our war preparation has befogged its economic origins, but all purposeful thinking about even the I. W. W.'s attitude towards the war must begin with a full and careful consideration of these origins.

"All the famous revolutionary movements of history gained their cause-for-being from intimate and unendurable oppression, and their behavior-in-revolt reflected the degree of their suffering. The chartist and early trade union riots in England, the revolution of 1789 in France, the Nihilists' killings in Russia, the bitter attacks on the railroads by the Grangers of the Northwest, the extremes into which the Anti-Saloon League propaganda has evolved, are a small part of the long revolt-catalogue of which the I. W. W. is the last entry. Each one of these movements had its natural psycho-political antecedents and much of the new history is devoted to a careful describing and revaluation of them. At some later and less hysterical date the I. W. W. phenomenon will be dispassionately dissected in somewhat the following way:

(1) There were in 1910 in the United States some 10,400,000 unskilled male workers. Of these, some 3,500,000 moved, by discharge or quitting, so regularly from one work town to another that they could be called migratory labor. Because of this unstable migratory existence the labor class lost the conventional relationship to women and child life, lost its voting franchise, lost its habit of common comfort or dignity, and gradually became consciously a social class with fewer legal or social rights than is conventionally ascribed to Americans. The cost of this experience was aggravated by the ability and habituation of this migratory class to read about and appreciate the higher social and economic life enjoyed by the American middle class.

(2) The unskilled labor class itself experienced a life not markedly more satisfying than the migratories. One-fourth of the adult fathers of families earned less than $400 a year, one-half earned less than $600. The minimum cost of decent living for a family was approximately $800. Unemployment, destitution, and uncared-for sickness was a monotonous familiarity to them.

(3) The to-be-expected revolt against this social condition was conditioned and colored by the disillusionment touching justice and industrial democracy and the personal and intimate indignities and sufferings experienced by the migratories. The revolt-organization of the migratories, called the I. W. W., failing, most naturally, to live up to the elevated legal and contract-respecting standards of the more comfortable trade union world, was visited by severe middle class censure and legal persecution.

"This sketch is fairly complete and within current facts. No one doubts the full propriety of the government in suppressing ruthlessly any interference by the I. W. W. with the war preparation. All patriots should just as vehemently protest against the suppression of the normal economic protest-activities of the I. W. W. There will be neither permanent peace nor prosperity in our country till the revolt-bases of the I. W. W. are removed, and till that is done the I. W. W. remains an unfortunately valuable symptom of a diseased industrialism."

The fourth paper, "Motives in Economic Life," represents the last piece of writing Carl Parker completed. This was read before the American

Economic Association in January, 1918, three months before his death. He was, of course, tremendously excited at the opportunity to get his new doctrines before a body of economists. After the paper he sent a joyous telegram back to California that it had gone vastly better than he had dared hope for. How eager he was to get his ideas in book form! He was working on this book until mediation duties in the Northwest took his entire time.

There was in the heart of Carl Parker, as there must be in the heart of many true scholars, more than the desire merely to add to the sum total of earthly wisdom. He possessed that quite understandable and altogether worthy belief that besides adding to the world's knowledge, he had something intellectual to give which would actually increase the larger happiness of men — could his theories be sensed by enough people to assure their application. Certain injustices loomed large to him — the maladjustment of present income distribution in a pecuniary order where money was of necessity to gratify most of normal instinct cravings; the unequal workings of the law (he never forgot at the time of his Federal investigation of the Wheatland Riot finding a friendless nineteen-year-old lad in a country jail who had been there eight months without any charge whatever against him, — his name not even down on any record. He had been hurled into jail in one of those God-fearing clean-ups when we rid society of all vestiges of the to us unpleasant and feel thereafter we can look our Maker complacently face to face. "Well done thou good and faithful servant!" How long the boy would have remained in his contaminous surroundings had Carl Parker not run across him no one knows.) And too he felt the yearning of the worker himself to understand the forces around and against him. He always kept a letter from a member of the Cooks and Waiters Union Local 295, written from Douglas, Arizona, in 1915:

Mr. Parker Prof of Economics State Univosity of Cal.

Dear Sir

You were in Phoenix last fall on industrial relations Between Capital & Labor I had the opertunity of hearing you once in Trades Councle Hall as I did not get to hear your full report on plan to settle Labour Disputes and on Industrial commissions I would like to know wether it is Posible for you to send me one of those charts or Practical Plans by whitch Labour Troubles can be avoided as I am only 1 among many Millions of peopple that has to

pay the Price of my rong Conceptions and understanding of life

I remain yours as student for Information

E. E. B.

Yet the debt he felt he owed was to no one class
— he labored to lift the veil of uncertainty and
doubt from his own eyes, and then share his findings with seekers after light be they rich or poor,
young or old, employer or employed. While in-
tellectually he might have to recognize classes in
our social structure, in his heart he knew none —
no distinctions. Except indeed between those
who were content to let creation drift — "God's
in his Heaven, all's well with the world" — who
held to a complacent aimless feeling of optimism,
who believed everyone got ahead in this country
who deserved to get ahead, — and those who felt
that now was the time to strain every intellectual
nerve in an honest, unembittered desire to understand the world, and each according to his abilities
to help in the struggle for more sanity, more
justice, more good-will. He blamed no one. He
tried to comprehend the forces at work which
made for certain conditions. He tried to understand the motives which led to certain types of
conduct. And, as expressed in his report to the

Governor on the Wheatland Riot, he pleaded that man should not be judged apart from his background, his environment. "Environment has its children as well as men."

Thus has one of his colleagues described Carl Parker's intellectual stand.[1] "There have very recently emerged in America a few men who might most appropriately be called the new frontiersmen. These men have the same simplicity, the same wander-spirit, and the same ruggedness that we so justly admire in the best of our older adventurers. But since the geographical frontier-line of America has become at least temporarily fixed on Pacific coasts, the new frontiersmen have sought the Hesperides in a new class-consciousness, or rather inter-class-consciousness. They have migrated not necessarily from their native states but away from many of the superstitions which bound them. The elusive and ever-moving frontier-line is now economic rather than geographical. But 'economic' is perhaps a vague and dangerous adjective because of its narrower connotations. These men have not migrated from one economic class into another. They have merely emancipated themselves from the idols

[1] Herbert E. Cory in University of California Chronicle, 1918.

and taboos of the class in which they were born
and reared, though with no intention of spurning
anything that is really noble in these old associations. On vital questions the new frontiersmen
take no pallidly non-partisan view. But they
choose their sides. Carleton H. Parker was one
of these new frontiersmen. He defied his foes and
he defied his friends. He aroused their anger and
he aroused their love. He was not too proud to
confess his ignorance in a day when so many men
and women deepen the perils of civilization by
assuming that oracular attitude which stills mo-
mentarily even their own murmuring fears. He
read consumedly but with increasing profit the
books of the bolder men who today seek light, as
Descartes sought light three hundred years ago
as a pioneer of a great reconstructive movement,
by accomplishing first of all a complete spiritual
house cleaning. Professor Parker moved with
tireless energy among the huts of lumberjacks, in
the depths of mines, in city labor councils, in the
withering heat of the hopfields at harvest time,
in the most intense class battles in California, in
Arizona, in Washington. He won the paternal
interest of a number of brave American scientists
who from different parts of the country have

sounded their warnings during the last ten years
to a population profoundly cursed with the 'op-
timistic squint.' In a word he recognized, what
all thoughtful men today must recognize, that the
chief hope for the salvation of western civilization lies in some sort of alliance between the labor
movement and the newly oriented sciences which
deal with the behavior of men, their modes of organization, their inherited unit-characters, and
their institutional habits. For this alliance, in
the interests of his country in its great crisis,
Carleton Parker worked and worked until, worn
out by incessant exertion in a storm center of
labor difficulties, he died untimely, consecrating
a precious life to American solidarity.

.   .   .   .

"The open-minded economist is forced today to
take the best account he can of the biological
sciences (particularly of heredity and of animal
behavior), of ethnology, of psychology, of philosophy (particularly those branches of philosophy
which today dub themselves 'the problem of consciousness,' 'the logic of science,' and 'the study
of values'). This great duty Carleton Parker
recognized and set himself with courage and enthusiasm to fulfill. . . . We must be content

here to emphasize the unique character of Professor Parker's contributions. He made substantial progress in standardizing the various conflicting inventories of human instincts (not unmindful of the dangers of lapsing back into a 'faculties psychology') and he sketched briefly but very suggestively the specifically economic significance of these instincts. And above all, he had thrown the searchlight of psychopathology on economic phenomena in a way which, despite the disputes among psychopathologists themselves, will assuredly prove the beginning of a very important contribution to the social sciences. Only those of us who knew something of his manuscripts and who sat under him week after week in his courses can appreciate how rapidly and broadly his mastery was coming when he gave his life to democracy. . . .

"Carleton Parker's most elaborate and trying experiences and investigations and most of his published writings dealt mainly with the unskilled workmen. For years Professor Parker fraternized with, remonstrated with, studied and wrote about our I. W. W., concerning whose bare name so many people had hardly heard six months ago. Professor Parker belonged to a group of radicals which searches for the roots of things with all the scientific acumen and technique at its command. These radicals are working fearlessly and tirelessly for the best interests of the United States. . . . Undoubtedly Carleton Parker's most permanent contribution to science and to his country was his amazing ability to turn all sorts and conditions of men and women from hedonists, cynics, sentimentalists, predatory egoists, and dilettantes into devoted workers for humanity. . . . For all the tragedy of his sudden death it may be said quite literally that his work has only begun. He has left behind him a host of men and women, old and young, employers, employees, students, ministers, lawyers, scientists, whose lives have been made vastly different by his life, who are determined to carry on work like his very much as he laid down the programme, who will carry it on with recurrent acknowledgements of indebtedness to him, and who love to quote as he loved to quote the words of Woodrow Wilson:

" 'We are in a temper to reconstruct economic society as we were once in a temper to reconstruct political society.' "

CORNELIA STRATTON PARKER.

I

TOWARD UNDERSTANDING
LABOR UNREST

A SHORT history will explain my thesis. In 1914 I was asked to investigate a riot among 2800 migratory hop pickers in California which had resulted in five deaths, many fold more wounded, hysteria, fear and a strange orgy of irresponsible persecution by the county authorities — and on the side of the laborers, conspiracy, barn burning, sabotage, and open revolutionary propaganda. I had been teaching labor problems for three years and had studied it in two American universities, under Sidney Webb in London, and in four universities of Germany. I found that I had no fundamentals which could be called good tools with which to begin my analysis of this riot. And I felt myself merely a conventional if astonished onlooker before the theoretically abnormal but manifestly natural emotional activity which swept over California. After what must have been a most usual intellectual cycle of first, helplessness, then conventional cataloguing, some rationalizing, some moralizing, and an extensive feeling of shallowness and inferiority, I called the job done.

By accident at this time I was loaned two books of Freud, and I felt after the reading that I had found a scientific approach which might lead to the discovery of important fundamentals for a study of unrest and violence. Under the stimution I read during a year and a half general psychology, physiology and anthropology, eugenics, all the special material I could find on Mendelism, works on mental hygiene, feeblemindedness, insanity, evolution of morals and character, and finally found a resting place in a field which seems to be best designated as Abnormal and Behaviouristic Psychology. My quest throughout this experience seemed to be pretty steadily a search for those irreducible fundamentals which I could use in getting a technically decent opinion of that riot. In grand phrases I was searching for the Scientific Standard of Values to be used in analyzing Human Behavior. In order to clarify my peculiar intellectual position I will make this additional statement regarding my trade.

Nearly all modern economics is a descriptive sub-science. It is concerned in the main with estimating the efficiencies of various instruments to produce goods, or services, or law and order, etc., without any important reference to the influence of any of these things upon the evolution of the human species. The training of a bird dog is full of infinitely more human attentions. This has allowed economics (which officially holds the analysis of labor problems) to devote itself almost entirely to the production of goods and to neglect entirely the consumption of goods and human organic welfare. The lip homage given by orthodox economics to the field of consumption seems to be inspired merely by the feeling that disaster might overcome production if workers were starved or business men discouraged. So while the official economic science tinkers at its transient institutions which flourish in one decade and pass out in the next, abnormal and behavioristic psychology, physiology, psychiatry, are building in their laboratories by induction from human specimens of modern economic life, a standard of human values and an elucidation of behavior fundamentals which we must use in our legislative or personal modification of modern civilization. It does not seem an over statement to say that orthodox economics has cleanly overlooked one of the most important generalizations about human life which can be phrased, and that is,

That human life is dynamic, that change, movement, evolution, are its basic characteristics.

That self expression, and therefore freedom of choice and movement, are prerequisites to a satisfying human state.

Modern economics tends to think in and talk of static states, the market price, an exchange value, constitutionality, reasonable freight rates, a just rate of interest. The old economic theory and its assumptions were fatally faulty in their simplicity, in their obvious practicality, in their easy usableness.

I have just completed a pilgrimage to various shrines within the human nature field, beginning with Veblen in Missouri and ending here in New England. The loot of this trip, modified by my personal intellectual bias is as follows:

Man, to quote John Dewey specifically and to condense the general theory of Thorndike, is a mosaic of original, uneradicable, and unlearned tendencies to action, an equipment of behavior unit characters. It matters little whether these begin psychically isolated from each other and numerous, or whether they begin with Brill's two basic instincts of hunger and sex, or Trotter's four instincts of self-preservation, nutrition, sex, and gregariousness, and then gain number by the numerous possible arithmetic combinations. As good a Freudian as Adolf Meyer, with a health-bringing constant contact with human laboratory stuff, said that he could not account for much in human behavior without postulating a man born with numerous fixed and unlearned tendencies to action. John B. Watson is ready to announce the successful isolation and description of five instincts through his remarkable experiments with new born babies. I personally looked on with astonishment, mixed with conventional moral indignation, while he forced an hour-old and wailing American infant to swing seven minutes by its one-handed grip on a pencil. A negro baby with a more recent and virile biological memory swung fourteen minutes.

Human action, shortly after birth, tends to find itself exercising along certain stereoptyped behavior channels, and so, to avoid that border land of pseudo-metaphysical speculation touching the parentage of these tendencies, I have selected for strict phrasing instead of "instincts," the words "unlearned tendencies to action" as describing the original physical baggage, the so-called instincts, which accompanies the remarkable anatomical contraption we have called man. However, I shall use "instincts" and "unlearned tendencies" as equivalent expressions.

My only attempt at any deductive theorizing regarding instincts is this: Given, that order and preparedness which variation and selection has guaranteed to that life on this earth which survives, it seems that as complex, intricate, and defenseless a machine as man's body would not be found turned loose in its highly dangerous environment without a guiding, a warning, a behavior system. It seems technically impossible to have expected a survival of the human species if, taking biological competition as it is, man had been forced to learn through trial and his errors a complete scheme of conduct. Therefore, it seems fair to deduce for man an unlearned bundle of instincts or tendencies having for the organism high survival value. Without these tendencies the human organism would have had a brief tragic struggle with its parasitic or flesh eating rivals, and man's participation in mundane affairs would have been the furnishing of important fossil re-

mains to some future sober congress of the sur-
viving earth species. Certainly, if we should
compare the high degree of weakness of physical
competition which man has developed in contrast
with his vertebrate and germ enemies, and also
in contrast with his own remote ape ancestors,
one could in retrospect see that the survival of the
human species must have had as a prerequisite a
rich and varied instinct equipment which removed
man from the necessity of learning a complete
scheme of behavior via the dangerous trial and
error method. The species without some unlearned and protective capacities would not have
lasted the instruction.

The importance to me of the following description of the innate tendencies or instincts lies in
their relation to my main explanation of economic
behavior which is:

First, that these tendencies are persistent, are far
less warped or modified by the environment than we
believe, that they function quite as they have for several hundred thousand years, that they as motives in
their various normal or perverted habit form can
at times dominate singly the entire behavior and act
as if they were a clear character dominant.

Secondly, that if the environment through any of the
conventional instruments of repression such as reli-

gious orthodoxy, university mental discipline, economic inferiority, imprisonment, physical disfigurement, such as short stature, hare lip, etc., repress the full psychological expression in the field of these tendencies, then a psychic revolt, a slipping into abnormal mental functioning, takes place, and society accuses the revolutionist of being either wilfully inefficient, alcoholic, a syndicalist, supersensitive, an agnostic, or insane.

I am willing to admit I am about to hang a psychological wreath about the neck of the rolling stone, the law breaker, the mentally unbalanced. As Trotter has said, if we should revamp our conventional idea of normality by a study of human evolution, there might be a sensational change in the general social character of the population of our institutions of detention. An inmate of an asylum in answer to the bromidic question, "Why are you here, you look all right?" said: "Lady, I'm in the minority, that's all." The minority membership runs true from St. Francis of Assissi to the MacNamaras. Perhaps one should stop to most seriously emphasize this concept of a new human normality and also to appreciate the handicap to discussion which comes whenever every analyzer at a round table has a very different brand of human normality in mind.

There is that theoretical one hundred per cent normality which is gained for individuals by free mobility plus full environmental equipment of persons and instruments and which results in a harmonious and full expression of his psychic potentialities. Since each vigorous experimentation under these conditions would generate wisdom in direct proportion to the experiment, I think that an evolutionary and also conventionally desirable progress could be prophesied as a result. This progress has no so-called idealistic goal or direction. It has merely a potentiality for more wisdom. Not being in possession of that wisdom, we today cannot prophesy its probable scheme of conduct.

A second normality would be produced by that human mobility and freedom, and that environment, which would give far more unconventional experimentation, far more wisdom, than we now have, but not the amount which would crack human nature by hurrying its change of mores too much, or destroy those institutions of civilization which could be modified with some hope of their higher usefulness. Conscious that man will change, if he is to change, to this compromise normality concept, it is such a normality that I have in mind when I use the term. It is in the end in the interests of such a new Darwinian normality that the following list of the innate and unsuppressable tendencies is presented. The list is a tentative and naturally an incomplete enumeration of those tendencies which we can, I think, safely use in a trial diagnosis of present day affairs and irregularities.

A tendency to be sexual and under stereotyped stimuli to follow a universally observed method of gratifying that desire.

To be hungry.

To think (to go over into multiform activity).

To experience mother-love, etc.

To be gregarious.

To be curious (to manipulate, to dissect, to experiment).

To fear.

To collect, to hoard, to gain and hold property.

To migrate, to be mobile.

To feel revulsion at confinement (cause of prison psychosis).

To dislike the unmeasured, the unlimited, to dislike to lie or die in the open.

To fight, to be near fighting, to call for the knock out, to be cruel, to be pugnacious.

To lead a group, a gang, a class, to be elected to political office.

To follow a leader.

To display, to be ostentatious, to be vain, to be unconventional in dress.

To be workmanlike, to show a quality sense, to show a harmony sense in self expression.

To hunt (the sex chase, persecution of the weaker, to bully).

To vocalize.

Watson has shown, I am confident, that an original tendency for instance, like grasping, can claim priority in the life story of man. He has experimented on children a minute old and his handling was, within practical reason, the first real nervous experience of the infant. He feels that such an act could be called the only first experience of the child, since the next act would be modified by the nervous system matured and changed by its important, if single, experience. This ignores the possibility that Watson will be able to deduce a prenatal habituation in grasping due to the fortuitous position of the infant in the womb which seems to favor the right in contrast to the left hand.

So, following the illuminating motor pattern theory of E. B. Holt, one can say that far back in the life of the child, such a complementary subtle influencing of not only every instinct by every other, but the influence of all past experiences upon the developing act in progress, forces one to contemplate each behavior act as the external manifestation of an inner-instinct-experience-agglomeration. The general character of an act thus analyzed seems to the uninitiated or mentally inert hopelessly accidental and complicated. So, to escape the labor of puzzling out the haze of a behavior man and also to avoid the burden of ordering one's own life after so demanding a plan, man turns with relief to the simple expedient of reducing the salvage in human beings to a soul and saving it in due and convenient time by the energy generated through hysteria. Billy Sunday should be the idol of lazy and bewildered ministers. Hence a father who has neglected his son for twenty years endeavors to correct the dissolute and diseased organism well beyond its plastic period by a "man to man" talk or by turning him indignantly out of the house. So a mother who has not informed her daughter of her sex disposition turns frantically to the psychiatrist; or an inefficient university teacher to examinations in order to stimulate.

Man seems to be psychically both a blend and a mosaic. An abnormal repression of one's innate tendency modifies to an important extent the method of gratification and the insistence for the gratification of every other tendency. Each act and its behavior can only be accurately described as being the visible indication of a sort of composite sentiment which includes in its basis every experience we have ever lived through, and added to this, the bundle of innate tendencies within us.

A short discussion of some of the conventional influencing of one innate tendency by another will illustrate. The innate tendency to think or meditate can be sex day dreaming or musing over railway rates. Its duration and character is largely dominated by the activity of our own innate tendency to be workmanlike. An innate gregarious tendency, Trotter maintains, must be accepted in order to explain our universal subservience to public opinion and convention. This innate subservience modifies our sex expression, our experimentation, our pugnacious satisfactions, our vanities, even our father and mother love. Veblen has said that a standard of workmanlike conduct influences profoundly the manner in which all innate tendencies find their gratification. The followers of Freud have written the sex instinct preponderantly into every human act. This is,

I think, a misuse of a structural truth. Every act-emotion has a strain of sex running through it as it has a strain of every other innate tendency. The quarrel with Freud's followers seems to be only one of over-emphasis. I do not think that life taken in the mass, or the newer psychological experiments, afford evidence for their emphasis. It affords, it is true, evidence for an emphasis vastly beyond anything that convention will allow. Freud is probably right also in estimating that convention's opposition is heavily re-enforced by those who for mixed reasons fear an exposé of their psychical state. Sex has so manifestly mixed itself up with migrations, war, vanity, leadership, fear, curiosity, etc., that one is forced to wage, in the name of observed fact, an incessant warfare with one's own religion, family mores, university utilitarianism and current literature. Nothing becomes the economic world so ill as their record under the touchstone of the sex problem. The fact that ninety per cent of the migratory workers have no women awakens no train of thought. Economists are apparently one with the Chicago Vice Commission, — the Sex Instinct can be abolished.

Leadership acts in the interests of a dozen other

manifest tendency-satisfactions. Authority gives to the tendency to be curious, to investigate, to wonder about, and speculate, not only tremendous evolutionary value but great preëminence among the tendencies striving for general dominance. It is the proclivity which has made so-called progress possible and its inhibition, as Trotter argues, through conservatism and orderly moulding of life, is the cause of well grounded pessimism about the future of the human race.

If these be the unlearned tendencies, how do they function? And perhaps if the problem be not too appalling, what is a full functioning, a complete psychological life? Since Freud, the pioneer in such an analysis, began with a description of manifest anti-normal functioning, the evidence is mainly in this field, and one is practically driven to paint the picture of a true normal life by the crude method of describing the opposite. At any rate the practice of first labor would be to free man from balkings and inhibitions. And then for the moment, trust like an idealist that the released human energy would muddle man to a conventionally nicer level. The innate tendencies, making up as they do the total motive power of man, gain an expression depending absolutely on the liberty afforded them by the environment and on the quality of the tools at hand. For sex, for migration, gregariousness, collecting, leadership, etc., there seem methods of satisfying which not only feel right and just to our experienced selves, but these methods seem to have a place in the scheme of conduct of biologically vigorous persons.

So we ascribe a high degree of normality to these methods of satisfying. In contrast to these in reality rare if desirable ways, are countless ways of gratification which are compromises between a fair approximation of this norm and a gratification so pitiful or so psychically costly or nauseatingly revolting or so egotistically brutal that much of orthodox religion is devoted to the simple task of either hiding these or damning them to death. Denied a normal expression one is said to sublimate the energy, evaporate it off through devotion to a different satisfaction. One is also said to compensate through a kindred substitute-activity for the thwarting of the direct instinct expression.

One of the great discoveries of Freud was that in early childhood all the psychical equipment is present and pressing for gratification, and that the highly repressive character of the conventional discipline for children guaranteed an immense number of minor and major thwartings and the attendant complexes. These complexes arise in such a manner as this: Little children have a universal and instinctive interest in manipulating anything they can get their hands on, in pulling it to pieces and looking at its insides. Toys in the hands of free children are soon reduced to their elements, the young of their pet animals die under their experiments. The fact that our own family cat had presented the household with an expected bunch of kittens came to me through the query of my four-year-old son as to why little kittens could not swim. Experiments of his on the brood of blind kittens in a horse trough had produced enligtening if fatal consequences. The results of balking innate dispositions of children are illuminated by the details of a case taken from the records of a New York psychiatrist (Brill). A small child born into a wealthy family was neglected from infancy by her parents. Her only relation with them was a daily interview with her mother in which the condition of her clothing was inspected and a nurse's recital of her breaches of discipline heard. The nurse told the mother one day of the child's breaking a valuable vase by pulling it off the table. The mother at that moment was nervous and annoyed by some other event and had burst out with unexpected fury. She whipped the child before the nurse. It was the first time she had ever touched the child. The child during the whipping had hysterically repeated over and over again, "I only wanted to see what was inside the vase." The nurse in order to stand well with the mother instituted a calculated system of activity repression for the child, and to gain enforcement of her rules, built up by threats and terrifying stories a horde of spirits and devils who inhabited the dark forbidden rooms or bric-a-brac. The child, for relief to her innate demands, began to build up phantasies and delusions. Frequently she would stand an hour or more looking out a window at a vacant lot. Later this nurse was discharged, and a loving and mystical old woman hired in her place. This person entered into the spirit world of the child with enthusiasm and the two developed this phantasizing, this habit fixation, into infinite detail. When later this nurse was discharged for intemperance the girl, then past adolescence, developed immediately a high irrationality, was very fearful, and suffered extreme night terrors. The psychiatrist found that the child had identified the nurse with her obsessional and perverted phantasy habit and that with her gone, life was an irresistible terror. The intemperate maid was rehired and an interview had with the mother in which the scientific results of her mother infidelity were enumerated. The mother is now trying to give to her daughter something of those experiences lost to her in her childhood and to become a satisfaction-feature of the child's life rather than a dreaded guilt-reminder, a repression-spectre who is to be hated, avoided and fooled. In lesser degree and with milder results this story is repeated in the lives of millions of children. If we should sympathetically take the tentative list of innate human proclivities here presented, and using them as norms investigate the infinite detail of the lives of one hundred children in the period between birth and their year of adolescence, we should uncover literally thousands of serious complexes and fixations. Mothers, fathers, teachers, ministers, playmates, the sophisticated street idler, all taken together Trotter's social censor — conventional society — gives the repressive force. Fear of punishment by parent or teacher, fear of public scorn, fear of a playmate's ridicule, fear of being caught kissing one's mother, fear of the policeman, of being uninvited, the educated fear of the darkness and its population of devils, fear of the unknown and the limitless, fear of a cheap funeral, fear of being out of style, fear of being off the band wagon, fear of not being right, all these give us our psychic hot points, our obsessions.

An interesting generalization can be made here. These guilt obsessions result almost universally in an inferiority phobia, a *"minderwertigkeit,"* a feeling of guilt. This inferiority-realization creates two types of reaction — either the person affected is weak kneed, submissive, yellow streaked, a backslider, a fair weather friend; or secondly, he becomes a strange creature who compensates for his inferiority by an aggressive ordering of his life as if he were imbued with the opposite character virtues. Among notable inferiority compensations of this class are:

Bragging of the timid.
Bravery of the physically small.
Cheerfulness of the dying (Tuberculosis Psychosis).
Washing mania of the immoral.
Orthodoxy of Rockefeller.
The vociferously "fair" to laborers.
Ostentatious interest of cotton mill owners in the welfare of the child workers.

The peace work of Carnegie in contrast to his Homestead strike policy.

Acquisition of the dyspeptic.

Dilettante intellectualism of the self-made.

Patriotism of the unheroic.

Generosity of the saloon-keeper to the poor.

By this devious path I come now to the character of evolution in the field of modern industrialism. Children of the middle class without doubt have a more unhealthy psychic life than those of the working class. But following the statistics of evident malnutrition, short school experience, and the abnormally high death rate of children of mill towns, our conventional mores have moved us to general if mild conviction that children of the working class are woefully badly off. It seems, however, that the necessary laxness of working home discipline, the decay among the working population of respect for conventional rules and law, the favorable opportunities for the children to quit school, the plasticity of the codes governing street social life, all work in an important manner towards allowing a relatively free and healthy psychic development of the children affected by it. Working mothers have not the time to enforce minutely the best current moral standards, for it takes much of the day's energies of the upper middle class mother to create by such an enforcement that atmosphere whose frequent and almost normal product is the above analyzed sexual and economic abnormalties.

However, at a later date in the life of these working class children, certain powerful forces in their environment, though they work on the less susceptible and less plastic natures of mature individuals, produce obsessions and thwartings which function at times, exclusively almost, in determining the behavior of great classes of the industrial population. The powerful forces of the working class environment which thwart and balk instinct expression are suggested in the phrases monotonous work, dirty work, simplified work, mechanized work, the servile place of labor, insecure tenure of the job, hire and fire, winter unemployment, the ever found union of the poor district with the crime district, and the restricted district with prostitution, the open shop, and labor turnover, poverty, the breadlines, the scrap heap, destitution. If we postulate some twenty odd unit psychic characters which are present under the laborer's dirty blouse and insistently demand the same gratification that is with painful care planned for the college student, in just what kind of perverted compensations must a laborer indulge to make endurable his existence?   A western hobo tries in a more or less frenzied way to compensate for a general all embracing thwarting of his nature by a wonderful concentration of sublimation activities on the wander instinct. The monotony, indignity, dirt and sexual apologies of, for instance, the unskilled worker's life bring their definite fixations, their definite irrational inferiority obsessions.   The balked laborer here follows one of the two described lines of conduct:

First, either weakens, becomes inefficient, drifts away, loses interest in the quality of his work, drinks, deserts his family, or,

Secondly, he indulges in a true type-inferiority compensation and in order to dignify himself, to eliminate for himself his inferiority in his own eyes, he strikes or brings on a strike, he commits violence or he stays on the job and injures machinery, or mutilates the materials; he is fit food for dynamite conspiracies. He is ready to make sabotage a part of his regular habit scheme.   His condition is one of mental stress and unfocussed psychic unrest, and could in all accuracy be called a definite industrial psychosis.   He is neither wilful nor responsible, he is suffering from a stereotyped mental disease.

If one leaves the strata of unskilled labor and investigates the higher economic classes he finds parallel conditions. There is a profound unrest and strong migratory tendency among department store employees. One New York store with less than three thousand employees has thirteen thousand pass in a year through its employ. Since the establishment in American life of "big business" with its extensive efficiency systems, its order and de-humanized discipline, its caste system, as it were, there has developed among its highly paid men a persistent unrest, a dissatisfaction and decay of morale which is so notable and costly that it has received repeated attention. Even the conventional competitive efficiency of American Business is in grave question. I suggest that this unrest is a true psychosis, a definite mental unbalance, an efficiency psychosis, as it were, and has its definite psychic antecedents — and that our present moralizing and guess-solutions are both hopeless and ludicrous. We blindly trust that a ten per cent wage increase will cure that breakdown which a sympathetic social psychiatrist might, if given all power, hope merely to alleviate. Other economic classes suffer from the limited outlet their environment affords — a narrow thwarted life drives unmarried women into France as nurses. Students, disappointed and balked by the impersonal and perfunctory instruction given in American universities, compensate by an enthusiasm over athletics and student activities which, if part expended in intellectual exercise, would revolutionize society. College athletics is a sort of psychic cure for the illness of experiencing a university education. The activity of many particularly placid people in the interests of peace might be identified as a compensatory and satisfying identification of their fearful selves with a desirable state of bloodshed. Many unmarried and repressed women gain a vicarious sex equivalent in a morbid interest in births, funerals, fires, and collecting things having sex symbolic value.

The most notable inferiority compensation in industrial life is the strike. The strike has two prerequisites, — a satisfactory obsession in the labor mind, and a sufficient decay in the eyes of labor of the prestige of social norms, to allow the laborer to make those breaches of law and convention which a well run strike of today demands. The violence of the strike varies directly with both the psychic annoyance due to the obsession

and with the extent of decay in the striker's eyes
of conventional mores. Veblen has shown how
modern machine technology gives a causal, de-
terministic bias to labor class thinking and how
this bias makes impossible the acceptance at face
value of the mystic, anthropomorphic pretensions
of law and business rights. These pretensions
seem fitted to endure only in a society experiencing a placid, unaroused and ox-like existence, or
in one where the prestige of law and order is maintained by a large professional army and a policy
of frightfulness not rendered inefficient by the inopportune presence of emotional religions.
Neither of these prerequisites is present in
America, so our strikes tend to reflect without
serious modification both the psychic ill-health
generated by the worker's experience, and the
rapid and interesting decay of the respect and
popularity of the law, the courts, property, and
the rich man. Trotter has described modern social revolt as the war between man stimulated by
his sore psychical experiences and the Power of
the Herd. This is but a Veblenesque description
of the strike.

My main thesis might be stated as a plea to
consider the states of conventional "Willfulness,"

such as laziness, inefficiency, destructiveness in strikes, etc., as ordinary mental disease of a functional kind, a sort of industrial psychosis. If we accept this approach then the cure for these menacing social ailments beckons to us from the field of abnormal and comparative psychology. We must, however, be prepared for a thorough mental house cleaning. Conventional thinking, conventional economics and its standards of value, are ruled out because they assisted in the promotion of evolutionary inefficiency. For instance, most economists glory in cheap and much food, cheap and much timber, cheap and good land, though it seems that these easy and unearned gifts have given the American part of the human race a psychic bias towards uncritical waste, an undisturbed liking for rapid and spectacular consumption, and a listlessness over questions of the ultimate problems of human survival, which make our intellectual processes curiously like those of primitive man.

The habituation of the higher constructive instinct in us has been slurred (except where they are narrowly concerned with production for waste) and the more genuinely indicative and more difficultly attained workmanlike qualities of contemplative thinking: art, poetry, evolutionary speculation, behavior study, philosophy, etc., are notoriously neglected and in possession of manifestly inadequate and unsatisfactory norms.

If I might be allowed to propose a program for reform this is such a program: Reform needs a militant minority, or to follow Trotter, a small Herd. This little Herd would give counsel, relief, and recuperation to its members. The members and the Herd will be under merciless fire from the convention-ridden members of general society. They will be branded outlaws, radicals, agnostics, impossible, crazy. They will be lucky to be out of jail most of the time. They will work by trial and study, gaining wisdom by their errors as Sidney Webb and the Fabians did. In the end, after a long time, parts of the social sham will collapse, as it did in England, and small promises will become milestones of progress.

From where, then, can we gain recruits for this minority? Two real sources seem in existence, the universities, and the field of mental disease speculation and hospital experiment. The one, the universities, with rare if wonderful exceptions, are fairly hopeless, the other is not only rich in promise but few realize how full in performance.

Most of the literature which is gripping that great intellectual no-man's land of the silent readers is basing its appeal and its story on the rather un-colored-up and bald facts which come from Freud, Trotter, Robinson, Dewey, E. B. Holt, Lippmann, Morton Prince, Pierce Bailey, Hart, Overstreet, Thorndike, Campbell, Meyer, Stanley Hall, Adler, White and Watson. It is from this field of comparative or abnormal psychology that the challenge to industrialism and the program of change will come.

But suppose you ask me to be concrete and give an idea of such a program. Take simply the beginning of life, take childhood, for that is where the human material is least protected, most plastic, and where most injury today is done. In way of general suggestion I would say, exclude children from formal disciplinary life, such as that of all industry and most schools, up to the age of eighteen. After excluding them, what shall we do with them? Ask John Dewey or read his "Schools of Tomorrow" or "Democracy and Education." It means tremendous, unprecedented money expense to insure an active trial and error learning activity, a chance to naturally recapitulate the racial trial and error learning experience, a study and preparation for those periods of life in which fall the ripening of the relatively late maturing instincts, a general realizing that wisdom can come only from experience and not from the Book. It means psychologically calculated childhood opportunity in which the now stifled instincts of leardership, workmanship, hero worship, hunting, migration, meditation, sex, could grow and take their foundation place in the psychic equipment of a biologically promising human being. To illustrate in trivialities, no father, with knowledge of the meaning of the universal bent towards workmanship, would give his son a puzzle if he knew of the Mecano or Erector toys, and no father would give the Mecano if he had grasped the educational potentiality of the gift to his child of $10 worth of lumber and a set of good carpenters tools. There is now enough loose wisdom around devoted to childhood, its needs, liberties, and experiences, both to give the children of this civilization their first evolutionary chance, as well as to send most teachers back to the farm.

In the age period of eighteen to thirty would fall that pseudo-educational monstrosity, the undergraduate university, and the degrading popular activities of "beginning a business" or "picking up a trade." Much money must be spent here. Perhaps few fields of activity have been conventionalized as much as university education. Here, just where a superficial theorist would expect to find enthusiam, emancipated minds, and hope, is found fear, convention, a mean instinct life, no spirit of adventure, little curiosity, in general no promise of preparedness. No wonder philosophical idealism flourishes and Darwin is forgotten. The first two years of university life should be devoted to the Science of Human Behavior. Much of to-day's biology, zoology, history, if it is interpretative, psychology if it is behavioristic, philosophy, if it is pragmatic, literature if it had been written involuntarily, would find its place here. The last two years could profitably be spent in appraising with that ultimate standard of value gained in the first two years, the various institutions and instruments used by civilized man. All instruction would be objective, scientific, and emancipated from convention — wonderful prospect!

In industrial labor and in business employments a new concept, a new going philosophy must unreservedly be accepted which has, instead of the ideal of forcing human beings to mould their habits to assist the continued existence of the inherited order of things, an ideal of moulding all business institutions and ideas of prosperity in the interests of scientific evolutionary aims and large human pleasures. As Pigou has said, "Environment has its children as well as men." Monotony in labor, tedium in office work, time spent in business correspondence, the boredom of running a sugar refinery, would be asked to step before the bar of human affairs and get a health standardization. Today industry produces goods that cost more than they are worth, are consumed by persons who are degraded by the consuming of them, destroying permanently the raw material source which science has painfully explained could be made inexhaustible. Some intellectual revolution must come which will de-emphasize business and industry and re-emphasize most other ways of self expression. In Florence around 1300, Giotto painted a picture and the day it was to be hung in St. Marks the town closed down for a holiday and the people with garlands of flowers and songs escorted the picture from the artist's studio to the church. Three weeks ago I stood in company with 500 silent, sallow-faced men at a corner on Wall Street, a cold and wet corner, till young Morgan issued from J. P. Morgan and Co.

and walked twenty feet to his carriage. We produce probably per capita one thousand times more in weight of ready made clothing, Irish lace, artificial flowers, terra cotta, movie films, telephones, and printed matter, than these Florentines did, but we have with our 100,000,000 inhabitants yet to produce that little town, her Dante, her Andrea del Sarto, her Michael Angelo, her Leonardo da Vinci, her Savonarola, her Giotto, — or the group who followed Giotto's picture. Florence had a marvelous energy-release experience. All our industrial formalism, our conventionalized young manhood, our schemitized universities, are instruments of balk and thwart, are machines to produce protesting abnormality, to block efficiency.

So the problem of industrial labor is one with the problem of the discontented business man, the indifferent student, the unhappy wife, the immoral minister, — it is one of mal-adjustment between a fixed human nature and a carelessly ordered world. The result is suffering, insanity, racial perversion, and danger. The final cure is gaining acceptance for a new standard of normality. The first step towards this is to break down the mores-inhibitions to free experimental thinking.

SAINT JOSEPH'S UNIVERSITY LIBRARY
GIFT RIDER

DATE: 7/17/91

DONOR: Dr. Miller

ACKNOWLEDGED:

VERIFICATION:

C-O:

AUTHORSHIP:

CN*

A.C.*

CALL NO.*

DATE or EDITION

*See: Disposition

DISPOSITION:

KEEP/FORMS
KEEP/REPLACEMENTS/A.C.
REFERENCE DESK
PERIODICALS
DISPLAY
VERTICAL FILE
AUDIO VISUALS
DOCUMENTS
BINDING
DISCARD

II

THE CASUAL LABORER

I. *The Wheatland Episode*

LABOR history, more than any other subdivision of economic history, seems to be written in terms of impressive events. In August, 1913, in the hop fields of Wheatland, California, such an event took place: an unusual strike, as strange as any in the annals of western labor. Men were killed, the country side cast into hysteria, the militia called out, and the State was made to realize overnight that San Francisco unionism was not the sum total of her labor problem. California long had known that nowhere in the country was there as unionized a city as San Francisco, that wages were high even as compared with the New York Building Trades, that the Exposition had been built as a closed shop, and that a candidate, be it for Governor, who was lukewarm regarding the policies of organized labor, had a remote chance of election. To Californians this for more than twenty years had been their labor question. With the dramatic entry of the hop pickers on the stage there began such a widespread and agitated discussion of the condition of the state's casual workers, that the two years of 1913 and 1914 will be known in western labor history as the "period of the migratory worker."

The story of the Wheatland hop pickers riot is as simple as the facts of it are new and naïve in strike histories. Twenty-eight hundred pickers were camped on a treeless hill which was part of the Durst ranch, the largest single employer of agricultural labor in the state. Some were in tents, some in topless squares of sacking or with piles of straw. Eight small toilets had been erected and four days use had made them revoltingly filthy. No toilets had been allotted to women. There was no organization for sanitation, no garbage disposal. The temperature during the week of the riot had remained near 105 degrees and though the wells were a mile from where the men, women, and children were picking, and their bags could not be left for fear of theft of the hops, no water was sent into the fields. A lemonade wagon appeared at the end of the week, later found to be a concession granted to a cousin of the ranch owner. Local Wheatland stores were forbidden to send delivery wagons to the camp grounds. It developed in the state investigation that the owner of the ranch received half of the net profit earned by an alleged independent grocery store which had been granted the "grocery concession" and was located in the center of the camp ground.

An examination of the wage system of this ranch for both the seasons of 1912 and 1913 showed an interesting phenomenon. Each day there existed four possible wage rates. If many hop pickers had drifted in by wagon and train and foot during the previous day, and as a result an unemployed crowd hung about the check window at sunrise, then 90 cents per hundred pounds was hung up as the piece price for hop picking. If there were unemployed still desirous for work even after this wage announcement, and a surplus hung about the window the following morning, it was the custom to lower the wages to 85 cents per hundred pounds. Like the immigrant at Ellis Island, the hop picker arrives at the job without a money reserve. The dictator of the wage policy of this ranch explained that if the pickers grew disgruntled at either rate of pay or the average

income and drifted away, leaving work checks un-
called-for, then the wage scale would be raised to
95 cents or even a dollar. There had been certain
days in the past, he said, when a labor exodus had
forced the price to as high as $1.10 before the
workers would flow in and allow the rate to sink
to a more profitable level. In order to counteract any wavering in allegiance to the job, 10 per
cent of the gross wages was held out by this ranch
to be paid to those who remained through the
season. The ranch owner argued that this was a
real bonus, because so many left before the season
was out that they, the deserters, fixed the real
average wage; therefore those who remained to
receive the ten per cent were paid just that
amount more than the average. In a private hearing before the Governor, an attempt to establish
whether a bonus should be taken from the wage
fund or the profit fund was without success. Possibly this failure illustrates a certain general confusion upon the issue. To uphold this wage
system it was necessary to advertise throughout
California and in southern Oregon and western
Nevada that everyone who applied on or before
the day picking was to begin could obtain a job.
It is difficult to estimate the vast number of mi-

gratory workers who make this ranch a short stopping place at some time in the five weeks of hop picking.

The pickers in August, 1913, were drawn from three sources. About a third came from California towns and cities, men and boys who form the great class of town casuals, and the wives and children from various stratas of the middle class. Another third were families from the Sierra foothills, quasi-gypsies, with carts or ramshackle wagons. The final third were the migratories, — the pure hobo, or his California exemplar, the "fruit tramp"; Hindus; and a large body of Japanese. There was much old-time California blood in this group, and even if the individuals had come upon evil economic days, their idea of personal dignity and their devotion to certain strange western "rights" had remained most positive. They began coming to Wheatland on Tuesday, and by Sunday the irritation over the wage scale, the absence of water in the fields, plus the persistent heat and the increasing indignity of the camp, had resulted in mass meetings, violent talk, and a general strike.

The ranch owner, a nervous man, was harassed by the rush of work brought on by the too rapidly ripening hops, and indignant at the jeers and cat-calls which greeted his appearance near the meetings of the pickers. Confused with a crisis outside his slender social philosophy, he acted true to his tradition and perhaps his type, and called on a sheriff's posse. What industrial relationship had existed was too insecure to stand such a procedure. It disappeared entirely, leaving in control the instincts and vagaries of a mob on one hand, and great apprehension and inexperience on the other.

As if a stage had been set, the posse arrived in automobiles at the instant when the officially "wanted" strike leader was addressing a mass meeting of excited men, women, and children. After a short and typical period of skirmishing and the minor and major events of arresting a person under such circumstances, a member of the posse standing outside fired a double barrelled shot gun over the heads of the crowd, "to sober them," as he explained it. Four men were killed, two of the posse and two of the strikers, the posse fled in their automobiles to the country seat, and all that night the roads out of Wheatland were filled with pickers leaving the camp. Eight months later two hop pickers, proven to be the leaders of the strike and its agitation, were convicted of murder in the first degree and sentenced to life imprisonment. Their appeal for a new trial was denied.

Dramatic because of the deaths and its suddenness, sordid in its details, in some way the episode caught and held the attention of the state. It is impossible to understand California's ensuing inspection on the subject of its peculiar labor problem without a description of the Wheatland episode. This brought the state to some degree of self-realization. The Federal Commission on Industrial Relations and the State Commission of Immigration and Housing turned their initial interest in the significance of the hop pickers riot to the problem of the migratory worker in the west thus dramatically introduced. The riot in the end served many purposes, one of which was to lend dignity to the I. W. W. in a very appreciable manner. Sympathy with syndicalism and ultra radical theories appeared in the most unexpected places. A group of women who had been identified with the most notable agitations in the California feminist movement went from trade union to union begging for funds to defend the indicted hop pickers. It was disclosed that many trade unionists in San Francisco were interested in the

I. W. W., some going so far as to have cards in both organizations. It was disclosed in the trial that certain suspects among the hop pickers had been held in jail many weeks without being charged or given a court hearing, a record of their arrest existing only on a so-called "secret blotter." This fact, in addition to an unexplainable participation of a private detective agency in the case, was a focus for very warm opinion. The county authorities' traditional treatment of vagrants and migratory workers with "no visible means of support" gave a sickening picture, and an uncomfortable hint of a vast amount of cruelty and injustice. Any romance which the Far West had thrown around a sheriff's posse was rudely stripped from the institution, and the prophecy was accepted that if the posse be the police power in any period of agricultural strikes and disorder, a large measure of dangerous inefficiency is assured. The most important result of the riot was the study of the economics of the labor field thus suddenly disclosed; and it is the results of this research to which we now turn.

II. *The California Casual*

California is a natural economic entity, insulated from the rest of the world by an ocean on the west, a desert south, and high mountains north and east. This gives a fair basis for isolating the labor problem to be considered under the present caption. The census shows the existence in the state of some 175,000 workers in the casual-using occupations. Of these, 72,157 are farm laborers "working out." A dependable estimate of the number of laborers in labor camps of the state at the time of maximum population is 75,000. The State Immigration Commission gathered statistics for 876 labor camps with a capacity of 60,813 workers. There has been a noteworthy industrial and agricultural specialization by districts in the state. Mining and the two diverse kinds of coast lumbering, i.e. the Sierra pine belt and the lower lying redwood belt, have given three detached labor fields. Agricultural California today is spotted with districts devoted to highly specialized and seasonal crops, running geographically from the oranges of the south through the walnuts of Santa Barbara, the raisins of Fresno, the artichokes of Half Moon Bay, the berries of Santa

Clara, to the early peach and the olive regions of the northern Sacramento Valley. Each town is a specialist and each Chamber of Commerce a "booster club" for a single product. This nature-ordained agricultural specialization is the basic cause of the existence of the California migratory worker. Another important factor is the circumstance that California for the last five years has been the scene of more railway and highway construction than any state in the West. Thus there was added to the local casuals a new element, the middle West railway laborer, the "construction work hobo." He has transplanted his personal habits and labor psychology into western soil without western adaptation.

In 1913-14 an investigation was carried on in California which utilized schedules covering 222 typical migratory workers, and from the resulting report the following generalizations appear well-based. Nearly half (48 per cent) were native Americans. The statistics of the Chicago Municipal Lodging House for 1910–12, covering 30,888 cases, of whom 60 per cent were estimated as migratories, give the percentage of "Americans" as 53.5. Of the California number investigated, 76 per cent were unmarried and 7.1 per cent had abandoned their wives. Four years of Chicago statistics show nearly 90 per cent unmarried. Of the 222, 47 per cent were under thirty years of age. A study in Chicago of 38,256 casuals in 1910–12 showed 44 per cent below thirty years of age. In California 33 per cent were between thirty and forty years of age, in Chicago, 27 per cent. Of the 30,888 examined in Chicago, 80 per cent were unskilled; 52 per cent of the California group admitted no trade training whatsoever. Of the Chicago group, but 21 per cent had been long enough in that city to establish a legal residence. Of the 222, 73 per cent had worked at their last regular job in some locality other than the one in which they were examined. Twenty-one per cent had had their last job outside the state. Forty-one per cent had been casual laborers less than six years, and 36 per cent between six and fifteen years. The per cent who admitted their intention of "floating" with no idea of looking for steady work was 67. Thirty-five per cent left their last job voluntarily. This hints at a conclusion which finds support in all the studies of the casual, the tramp, or the vagabond: that casualty begets a labor type permanently under normal. There is today sufficient evidence from various quarters to make this grave charge against seasonal work. For instance, in Belgium the statistics of admissions in 1908 to The Wortel Beggars Depot shows 1,222 committed for the first time, 435 for the second, 261 for the third, 163 for the fourth, and 717 for the fifth time or oftener.

Some of the more intimate statistics of the California group are suggestive: 22 per cent had belonged to a lodge; 29 per cent had been members of a Protestant Church, 18 per cent of the Catholic; 48 per cent gave no preference for a political party, yet 37 per cent advocated the complete destruction of the present political system. Despite the Wheatland riot and the extensive propaganda of the I. W. W. among this very labor class, but 8 per cent belonged to that organization. Forty-one per cent had ceased writing or maintaining any connection with relatives, and 86 per cent said no one was dependent upon them. Somewhat similar evidence is the fact that out of thirty suicides in the men's cheap lodging houses in San Francisco, in the month of December, 1913, but two left behind any word as to their source or relatives. The schedule examiners reported that 74 per cent were in good or fair physical condition, and 24 per cent sick. The Chicago statistics cover-

ing 130,053 cases reported 84.8 per cent "able-
bodied." Seventy-seven per cent of the 222 in
California were alcoholic, and 26 per cent admitted a jail record. The Department of Education of Stanford University tested two hundred
unemployed of the migratory labor class and almost an even 25 per cent were found feeble-
minded. Binet tests made in 1913 by the Economic Department of Reed College, Portland,
covering 107 cases taken from the unemployed
army showed the percentage of feeble-minded to
be 26.

A California state official of long technical experience, whose duties bring him in direct contact
with the young vagrant, believes that he has the
data to prove a widespread practice of homo-
sexuality among the migratory laborers. Investigation reports of a most dependable and technical nature show that in California lumber camps
a sex perversion within the entire group is as developed and recognized as the well known similar
practice in prisons and reformatories. Often the
men sent out from the employment agencies are
without blankets or even sufficient clothing, and
they are forced to sleep packed together for the
sake of warmth. Investigations are beginning to

show that there are social dangers which a group of demoralized, womenless men may engender under such conditions of greater menace than the stereotyped ill effects of insanitation and malnutrition.

III. *The Labor Camps and the Labor Turnover*

An investigation of the labor camps of the state was carried out in the summer of 1914 by the State Commission of Immigration and Housing under the direction of the present writer. Eight hundred and seventy-six camps were examined in which at some time in the summer 60,813 men were to be housed. Of these camps 297 (34 per cent), holding 21,577 workers, were pronounced in good condition; 316 (36 per cent), housing 22,382 men, fair; and 263 (30 per cent), housing 16,854 men, were so insanitary and destitute of essentials that they were entered as bad. In this investigation "fair" was below the minimum established by the State Board of Health. Of the berry camps investigated, 68 per cent had toilets statistically noted as "filthy." The toilets were in this same condition in 37 per cent of the fruit camps, 69 per cent of the grape camps, 38 per cent of the highway camps, 62 per cent of the 135 hop camps, 42 per cent of the lumber camps (though they could be described as permanent in many cases), 37 per cent of the mining camps, and 61 per cent of the ranch camps. The large corporation made an interesting break in this recital, for but 24 per cent of the railway camps were "filthy"; and in the oil fields, where Standard Oil and The Union Oil Company are largely in control, the percentage was 27. In 29 per cent of the construction and 25 per cent of the highway camps there were no toilets whatever. For all the 876 camps, 13 per cent had no toilets, 31 per cent maintained filthy toilets, 20.4 per cent fairly sanitary, 23.4 per cent sanitary and fly screened. Among all camps 40 per cent provided no bathing facilities at all, 39 per cent offered tubs or showers. Of the 537 labor camps using horses, 27 per cent allowed the manure to accumulate in the vicinity of the kitchen and mess tent. Thirty-five per cent of the kitchen and mess tents had no screens. Twenty-five per cent of the camps had no garbage disposal, the kitchen refuse being allowed to accumulate indefinitely. It is a proverb in the health service of the two great valleys that every labor camp has its typhoid carrier. Certain fruit towns expect their ten cases of typhoid per year.

It will be seen that the camp conditions at Wheatland constituted no isolated case. The early California population was a pioneer community and their complete acceptance of individualism gave little room for social realizations. This doctrine remains the current philosophy of the country districts, and despite the statewide influence of the social legislation of the Johnson administration, the inherited psychology of the employer of casual labor remains the same.

Resistance by the worker to an employer's labor policy takes one of two forms: either an open and formal revolt, such as a strike; or an instinctive and often unconscious exercise of the "strike in detail," — simply drifting off the job. The latter phenomenon is called by the employers "undependable labor," and ideas concerning this willful unreliability constitute the layman's usual version of the California labor problem. In the light of the recent investigations it would appear that the California employer obtains the labor to whom his conditions of employment are attractive. A study first of the "strike in detail" in the state is convincing.

Statistics were obtained from the books of the Southern Pacific and Northwestern Pacific, the two systems carrying on the most important railway construction in the west.

NORTHWESTERN PACIFIC

In a camp called the "Tunnel Camp," during the five months from January to May, 1914, 529 men worked 7414 days, an average of 14 days per man. Following are the statistics in detail:

Jan.	133	men	worked	2169	days,	average	16.3	days per man.
Feb.	107	"	"	1554	"	"	14.5	" " "
Mar.	138	"	"	1471	"	"	10.6	" " "
Apr.	90	"	"	1153	"	"	12.8	" " "
May	61	"	"	1067	"	"	17.5	" " "

In the "Grade Camp" of the same company adjoining the "Tunnel Camp," during the seven months from June to December, 764 men worked 7723 days, an average of 10.1 days per man.

June	68	men	worked	825	days,	average	12.1	days per man.
July	82	"	"	765	"	"	9.3	" " "
Aug.	73	"	"	944	"	"	13.3	" " "
Sept.	56	"	"	850	"	"	15.2	" " "
Oct.	171	"	"	1599	"	"	9.3	" " "
Nov.	166	"	"	1612	"	"	9.7	" " "
Dec.	146	"	"	1128	"	"	7.6	" " "

In the year 1913 the two adjoining camps had employed 1293 men working 15,137 days, an average of 11.7 days work per man.

Southern Pacific

In the "Grade Camp" of this company, statistics covering March 10 to July 8, show 480 men working 4145 days, an average of 8.6 days per man.

Mar.	10 days,	74	men worked	250	days.			
Apr.		136	"	1262	"	average	9.3	days.
May		180	"	1459	"	"	8.0	"
June		164	"	1424	"	"	8.7	"
July	8 days,	68	"	234	"			

These figures bear out the employment agency proverb that there are three crews of men connected with the job, one coming, one going, one on the job.

A big dried fruit packing firm in Fresno reported that to keep up a skilled crew of 93 men, 41 per week had to be hired throughout the season. A large ranch with a fruit season of nine weeks reported a monthly turnover of 245 per cent. One power house construction job in the Sierras gave figures showing that to maintain a force of 950, over 1500 men a month were shipped to them.

It seems that when a laborer has earned a sum which road tradition has fixed as affluence, he quits. This sum is known as a "jungle stake," and once it is earned the hobo discipline calls upon the casual to resort to a camp under a railroad bridge or along some stream, a "jungle," as the vernacular terms it, and live upon this "stake" till it is gone. Thereupon he goes north to a new maturing crop. Weeks spent among the casuals by two investigators lead them to attach great importance to this custom. In the words of a report, "The sum which usage prescribes that a jungle stake should be, taken in relation to the wage in the district, fixes the casual's endurance on the job. Today between ten and fifteen dollars is a proper stake." The statistics of the 222 California casuals examined show that but 29 per cent left their last job because work gave out. Taking into calculation both the tendency to drift away from a fairly permanent job, as shown by the construction work figures, and also the normal short duration of the fruit or harvesting work, such generalizations as the following, gathered by the investigators, seem to be dependable. The duration of a job is:

In lumber camps	15–30	days
" construction work	10	"
" harvesting	7	"
" mining	60	"
" canning	30	"
" orchard work	7–10	"

IV. *Winter Unemployment; the Revolt*

California is a state of summer employment. The seasonal activity of the canneries, the state's principal industry, illustrates this fully. In August, 1909, California canneries employed 16,047; in February, but 2781. Of the 150,000 migratory workers employed in the summer, a mass of direct and indirect information indicates that fully 100,000 face sustained winter unemployment. Driven out of the lumber and power construction camps and mines of the Sierras by the snow, out of highway camps by the regular winter shut down, and out of agriculture by its closed winter season, with a winter's stake estimated to be on the average $30, these tens of thousands "lie up" for from five to six months in the cities of the coast. A San Francisco canvas of the ten and fifteen cent lodging houses and the cheap hotels of the foreign quarter, made in December, 1913, showed that over forty thousand were "lying up" in that city. A Los Angeles estimate gave twenty-five thousand; Sacramento showed approximately three thousand; and important additions came from Stockton, Fresno, and Bakersfield. The winter of 1913 was a hard one for the lodging house man. His stake was small, and by October there were hungry men on the San Francisco streets and talk of a bread line. One of those odd creatures who inhabit the border land of labor, "General" Kelly, appeared, and in two weeks had organized an unemployed "army" whose enlistment soon reached two thousand. The recruits were a fair cross section of the thousands of migratories lying up in the city: those who were penniless and evicted from lodging houses, the younger gentry looking for adventure, the quasi-yegg looking for disorder, the border line defectives attracted by the military form, and lastly the normal casuals weary of monotonous privation. After a few weeks the inaction caused the more restless and able to drift away. By December, through this segregation, the "army" had become a human scrap heap and the wet and disconsolate camp on a vacant lot a social caricature. With doubtful generosity the city turned over to the army a vacant building near the City Hall. The use of this building is best described in the words of an investigator of the State Immigration and Housing Commission:

"The building runs from Market Street to City Hall Avenue, containing stores on the ground floor and fifty rooms of the Marshall Hotel on the second floor. Both the stores and the hotel have been dismantled and are vacant.

"According to instructions, your investigator arrived at the building at 11:30 P. M., Wednesday, February 18. There was a very heavy rain falling at the time and the men were pouring into the place at all the entrances. In the store, No. 1500 Market Street, 132 men were already sleeping side by side in rows along the floor, and several were standing by the stove. These latter were soaking wet, and a volume of steam was arising from their clothing. The air of the place was foul and stifling, all the doors and windows being closed in order to shield the sleepers from the cold air. Newspapers constituted the bedding of the sleepers. In the next vacant store were 187 men sleeping under like conditions.

"In the store which occupied the City Hall Avenue corner were 211 men. Here the men were sleeping upon the window platforms and so closely packed upon the floor as to make passage between them impossible. Seventeen men occupied the floor space of the main entrance of the up-stairs section, leaving barely enough room for persons to get through the doors. Three men were sleeping on the middle stairway landing. Lying on the floor of the upper hallways of the hotel were 138 men, all using newspapers for bedding. The men lay with their clothes on, with the exception of their shoes, which were utilized for pillows. There are 50 rooms on the second floor, and they averaged 14 men on the floor of each room. — Some of the rooms were so closely packed with men that it was impossible to open the door. They were lying in every shape and direction upon the floors of every passage and hallway of the house. In round numbers there were 700 men in the upper stories and over 500 in the vacant stores of the ground floor, a total of over 1,200 men with a constant stream of new-comers. A few men were standing in the shelter of the doorways, and in conversation they stated that they were driven out of the building by the odor and vermin. One of these men had been a resident of San Francisco for 20 years, and stated that this is his first experience of being without a bed and meal. He further stated that people he knew were unable to aid or give him credit until he obtained work. Another man, who is a discharged U. S. Army man, stated that he was living in a tent with Company M of Kelly's Army at Fifth and Mission Streets, and had come over to seek shelter owing to the heavy rain, but that he was going back to stay in the tent in preference to accepting the city's hospitality. This man accompanied the investigator through the Marshall Hotel. Lying directly at the head of the main stairway was a Mexican in the last stages of consumption. He was coughing and spitting all over the floor in his vicinity, the sputum making a disgusting and sickening sight. Men could be heard coughing in all parts of the building, and a number were sleeping in their rain-soaked clothing. The air was putrid and left a nauseating odor upon contact with the fresh air."

A few weeks later the Army began its demoralized march on the National Capital. It left San Francisco by ferry, landed in Oakland, was passed rapidly by armed Oaklanders through the city on to Richmond. Here the mayor of that exasperated town organized transportation and passed the hungry legion on to Sacramento by train. This town, after a day of fruitless cogitation, descended on the camp with pick handles and fire hose, drove the army across the river, and burned the blankets and camp equipment. Guards with rifles kept the bridge. The writer had the oppor-

tunity of remaining most of four days with this
now broken and dispirited body of men, studying
some fifty-odd closely. They were willing to talk,
many being in a highly excited and uncontrolled
state. Over half, through either long malnutrition
and privation, or through constitutional defects,
had reached an undeniably abnormal mental condition. There were defectives even among the
"officers," and much of their "strategy" against
the businesslike riflemen at the bridge was curiously like the scheming of small boys. The suffering and helplessness, the pitiful inefficiency of
this broken mob, the bitter humor of the feeble
military form to which it still clung, made the
entire picture an economic cartoon. It was impossible to be there and not get a vivid impression
of a class inferior, unequal, and with fewer rights
than normal American tradition seems to promise
to its citizens.

Within three weeks the Army, rained on and
starved out, melted away, and its members joined
that restless migration into which the first spring
days had stirred the lodging house population.
The Army's psychology had dissolved into the
larger psychology of the migratory 150,000, and
its winter's experience added to that collection of

strange complexes which make up the California casual's mob mind.

There is here, beyond a doubt, a great laboring population experiencing a high suppression of normal instincts and traditions. There can be no greater perversion of a desirable existence than this insecure, under-nourished, wandering life, with its sordid sex expression and reckless and rare pleasures. Such a life leads to one of two consequences: either a sinking of the class to a low and hopeless level, where they become through irresponsible conduct and economic inefficiency a charge upon society; or the result will be revolt and guerilla labor warfare.

The Wheatland strike was the latter. This was engineered by the I. W. W.; and though there were but a handful of members and a single leader at the Durst ranch, the strike was momentous in results. The trade unions themselves have given but perfunctory notice to the migratory laborer. Though the skilled railway employees are completely unionized, their interest has not extended to the railway construction workers, whose living and working conditions are utterly deplorable. California, an investigation showed, has between 4500 and 5000 active members of the I. W. W.

Up to the Wheatland affair their energy in the west had gone into free speech fights, notably at Fresno and San Diego. Since Wheatland they have devoted themselves entirely to organizing the migratory laborer. The destructive efficiency of the I. W. W. strike tactics, that of "direct action" and sabotage, was shown in the organized hop strike of 1914, though the strike failed. Even in the spring of 1915 barn and kiln burnings occured in the hop fields up and down the state, — a back fire of the riots of 1913. It is not difficult to understand the light allegiance to law and order, to the sanctity of property, which is an outstanding characteristic of this group. Much of their so-called syndicalistic philosophy analyzes down to a motive of resentment. Investigators report that sabotage and "putting the machine out of business" are the topics to which the road meetings turn. The group in all its characteristics is the poorest of raw material for labor organization. Shifting, without legal residence, under-nourished as a universal rule, incapable of sustained interest, with no reserve of money or energy to carry out a propaganda, they cannot put forth the very considerable energy which cooperation demands. Their numerous strikes in

California have been but flashes of resentment, and when their leaders in 1914 planned a great picketing of all the hop fields of the Sacramento valley, they found that their pickets after a week of patience began to slip onto freight trains and disappear to the south. The needed two thousand dwindled to a handful and the "great strike" flickered out. Hopes are high for the 1915 season; agitation is rife, and numerous fires to date give evidence of "direct action" already carried out on the part of the I. W. W. It remains to be seen how far the 1915 tactics of the organization will embarrass the agricultural employers of California, but the word has gone out that "no crop is to be harvested" until the indicted hop pickers, referred to in connection with the Wheatland affair, are freed.

As a class, the migratory laborers are nothing more nor less than the finished products of their environment. They should therefore never be studied as isolated revolutionaries, but rather as, on the whole, tragic symptoms of a sick social order. Fortunately the psychologists have made it unnecessary to explain that there is nothing willful or personally reprehensible in the vagrancy of these vagrants. Their histories show that, starting with the long hours and dreary winters of farms they ran away from, through their character-debasing experience with irregular industrial labor, on to the vicious economic life of the winter unemployed, their training predetermined but one outcome. As the Harvard biologist words it, nurture has triumphed over nature, the environment has produced its type. Difficult though organization of these people may be, a coincidence of favoring conditions may place an opportunity in the hands of a super leader. If this comes, one can be sure that California would be both very astonished and very misused.

III

THE I. W. W.

Any economic problem arising in the United States today is seen in a vivid setting of war expediency. The particular national danger to which the population is becoming increasingly sensitive colors every issue, social, economic, or moral, and the old logical approaches to them are rapidly going into the discard. Today prostitution, drink, and the free and easy American consumption of food and goods have been assailed with a vehemence and impatience astounding when compared with the gentle analyses in vogue a few years ago. This tendency gives the consideration of such a phenomena as the I. W. W. a dual nature, — first, the now dominant one of the I. W. W. in relation to the war psychology of America; and second, the I. W. W. in relation to the stable sweep and evolution of American industrialism. The intensity of the war temper which plays about the I. W. W. makes it very difficult to advance an analysis of a scientific nature touching even this latter relationship. Except in the form of complete and unconditioned denunciation, interest in this American manifestation of syndicalism is taboo. The Federal Government has within very recent weeks judged the I. W. W. as a menace to America's preparedness in war, and the union's leaders are either in prison or jeopardy. This positive action by the Department of Justice has so emphasized the relation of this union to the worries and expediencies of our war state that the I. W. W. as an economic problem has practically disappeared. But since the war-time behavior of the I. W. W. finds its only psychological explanation in its economic environment and experiences, the latter and tabood relationship must be the major concern of this article.

Another unappreciated consideration might be noted in passing. The domination of the American press over the form and method of publicity has given Americans a deep-seated bias in favor of a vivid and dramatic presentation of all problems, economic or moral. The rather gray and sodden explanation of any labor revolt by reference to the commonplace and miserable experi-

ences of the labor group would lack this demanded
vividness. Just as the French enjoyed the mean
stories of the debased life of the petty thief when
framed up and titled "A Picture of the Parisian
Apache," so the casual American demands white
hoods and mystery for the Kentucky night riders
and a dread, sabotage-using underground appari-
tion for the I. W. W. Some important portion of
I. W. W. terrorism can be traced directly back to
the inarticulated public demand that the I. W. W.
news story produce a thrill.

The futility of much conventional American
social analyzing is due to its description of the
problem in terms of its relationship to some relatively unimportant or artificial institution. Little
of the current analyses of strikes or labor violence
uses the basic standards of human desire and intention which control these phenomena. A strike
and its demands are usually praised as being law-
abiding, or economically bearable, or are con-
demned as being unlawful, or confiscatory. These
four attributes of a strike are important only as
incidental consequences. The habit of Americans
thus to measure up social problems to the current,
temporary, and more or less accidental scheme of
traditions and legal institutions, long ago gave

birth to our national belief that passing a new law or forcing obedience to an old one was a satisfying cure for any unrest. The current analysis of the I. W. W. and its activities is an example of this perverted and unscientific method. The I. W. W. analysis which has given both satisfaction and a basis for treating the organization runs as follows: The organization is unlawful in its activity, un-American in its sabotage, unpatriotic in its relation to the flag, the government, and the war. The rest of the condemnation is a play upon these three attributes. So proper and so sufficient has this condemnation analysis become that it is taboo to reapproach the problem. But now our internal affairs are so obviously out of gear that any comprehensive scheme of national preparedness would demand full and honest consideration be given to all forces that determine the degree of American unity, one force being this tabooed organization.

It would be best here to announce a more or less dogmatic hypothesis to which the writer will steadfastly adhere and which is: human behavior is the rather simple, arithmetic combination of the inherited nature of man and the environment in which his maturing years fall. Man will behave according to the hints for conduct which the accidents of his life have stamped into his memory mechanism. A slum produces a mind which has only slum incidents with which to work, and a spoiled and protected child never rises to aggressive competitive behavior, simply because its past life has stored up no memory imprints from which a predisposition to vigorous life can be built. The particular things called the moral attributes of man's conduct are conventionally found by contrasting this educated and trained way of acting with the exigencies and social needs or dangers of the time. Hence, while his immoral or unpatriotic behavior may fully justify his government, standing in some particular danger which his conduct intensifies, in imprisoning or abolishing him, this punishment in no way either explains his character or points to an enduring solution of his problem. Suppression, while very often justified and necessary in the flux of human relationship, always carries a social cost which must be liquidated and also a back-fire danger which must be insured against. The human being is born with no innate proclivity to crime or special kind of un-patriotism. Crime and treason are habit activities educated into man by environmental influences favorable to their development. There is one current objection to the above reasoning, and that is the opportunist one that this psychological explanation softens society's criticism of the act, say in this case sedition, and makes difficult its suppression. This may in fact take place, but since it is a result of the transitory state of affairs itself, it does not then justify the abolition of proven and scientific methods of analysis. Also, since any preparedness which can be relied upon in the coming dangerous years of our war participation must be based on fact calculation and not the loose and pseudo-hysterical emotions of desire, there is more need of proven scientific methods of social analysis than America has yet felt. The modern psychological study of behavior makes it impossible to view an I. W. W. as a mobile and independent agent, exercising free will and moral discretion. The I. W. W. is the result of a social admixture; he is a more or less finished product and any explanatory analysis should deal and deal alone with the antecedent experiences which produce in a most natural and every-day manner those practiced habits which we describe as "being an I. W. W." Syndicalism is then like patriotism or pacificism, a condition of mind.

There have been recently in the state of Washington mass meetings, private and public, devoted to the problem of the I. W. W. In one informal meeting a lumber mill operator of long experience advanced a policy of suppression, physical violence, and vigilante activity. A second operator, listening, observed, "If you lost your money, you would be the best I. W. W. in the state." It was this identity of mind which struck the second operator. It is accurate and also obvious to say that the upper reaches of business and society possess its I. W. W. The state of mind characterised by ruthlessness, high egotism, ignoring of the needs and helplessness of much of society, breaks out at different social levels under different names, but the human elements and even much of the vocabulary remains the same.

It must be reiterated that any attempt to use, at this particular day in our history, modern behavioristic psychology in an analytic way is not only under taboo but has resulted in an immediate persecution of the scientist who so offends. A certain editor in Yakima, in the State of Washington, has been known beyond his state limits for his strong and individual editorial policy. His editorials are more widely quoted than those of any paper in the state. This editor inadvertently put the I. W. W. horror to the practical test by interviewing some fifty I. W. W.'s interned in a Yakima jail. These individuals had held the Yakima Valley in terror and local feeling made lynching and the most extreme of violence not only possible, but incidents of the most reasonable expectancy. The editor observed in an editorial the following day, that the I. W. W. were much like the agricultural workers he had known all his life. Their desires were similar, and the details of their complaints touching the life they led were worthy of sympathetic investigation. They were not even, he thought, incorrigibly unpatriotic. He thought that he could even trust some of them. These observations almost resulted in an immediate ostracising of the editor. His method of analysis had been a very fair, if rough and ready, approximation of that used by modern dynamic psychology.

The interesting contradiction that these modern replicas of ancient intolerance and persecution will be carried through by a people sincerely ready to sacrifice kin and wealth in the cause of liberty, becomes no difficult problem to analyse and explain. Little has been written or made current to show how open to phobia and mob suggestion a nation is which, accustomed and set in the habits of peace and all-occupying business ends, has the props of this life suddenly cut out from under it. In a daze America has seen conscription come, prices fixed, industrial plants commandeered, freedom of speech modified. This is not an overturning of merely an unimportant feature of American life, it is the negation of nearly the entire Kultur of the nation. The habit and order of every-day thinking is made inefficient and inapplicable. While outwardly "business as usual" seems to an extent enforced, inwardly and in the hitherto secure mental background is chaos and the potentiality for almost any kind of irresponsible reasoning. Even in the rather secure social retreats of small town life take place, for instance, bursts of spy hunting, so cruel and in such variance with all the ideas of fairness and control which had been long accepted as American virtues, that one sees how adrift and helpless the psychological ship can become. Josiah Royce has said that America's nation-danger was her openness to mob suggestion. Her century of service as an immigrant melting pot carried its costs, and it was beyond reason to expect to see rise, from a scramble of transplanted nationalities, who had broken with their traditional religions, their rules of dress, morality, and political life, a nation which, in Ross' words, possesses a sturdy prophylactic against the hysteria of mob movement. The I. W. W. can be profitably viewed only as a psychological by-product of the neglected childhood of industrial America. It is discouraging to see the problem today almost exclusively examined regarding its relation to patriotism and conventional commercial morality.

The heart of the current condemnation of the I. W. W. is that it is a viciously unpatriotic organization. The writer of this article made a special investigation upon the above issue among the I. W. W. leaders. He pointed out that our nation was fighting a nation which suppressed free speech, not only opposed a free individualism, but moulded a citizen's mind to suit the particular and competitive needs of the state, and if it subjected us, would bloodily suppress just such disquieting agencies as the I. W. W. Methods of discipline would be turned back a hundred years to the ancient system of gaining citizenship unity through fear, and these policies would be enforced by a harsh military organization, flushed and confident from its victory. This presentation was invariably met by the I. W. W. leaders with a recital that for them there was only one war, and that the class war between the "master class" and the "slaves." It was, they argued, purely incidental whether a German or an American ruled the political machinery. It made even less difference whether the industrial master were a German or American. The class war was without national lines.

In answer to the argument that a bad political system might postpone in an important way the evolution they desired in class conflict, the leaders decried the importance of war and its political results. They quoted with astonishing facility the rises in the cost of meats, textiles, shoes, and so on. Their figures proved to be accurate. They had circulated through their lectures the fact that steel plates had risen from $26.50 a ton in 1913 to $200 in 1917, and the story of the increase in the surplus earnings of United States Steel, Bethlehem Steel and the powder companies. This they joined to a dissertation on the increase of farm tenancy. Presumably they were better acquainted with American social statistics than the academic class in which the writer lives. It is perhaps of value to quote the language of the most influential of the I. W. W. leaders.

"You ask me why the I. W. W. is not patriotic to the United States. If you were a bum without a blanket; if you had left your wife and kids when you went west for a job, and had never located them since; if your job had never kept you long enough in a place to qualify you to vote; if you slept in a lousy, sour bunkhouse, and ate food just as rotten as they could give you and get by with it; if deputy sheriffs shot your cooking cans full of holes and spilled your grub on the ground; if your wages were lowered on you when the bosses thought they had you down; if there was one law for Ford, Suhr and Mooney, and another for Harry Thaw; if every person who represented law and order and the nation beat you up, railroaded you to jail, and the good Christian people cheered and told them to go to it, how in hell do you expect a man to be patriotic? This war is a business man's war and we don't see why we should go out and get shot in order to save the lovely state of affairs which we now enjoy."

The argument was rather difficult to keep productive because that rather material prerequisite to patriotism, i.e. gratitude, seemed wanting in their attitude towards the American government. Their state of mind could only be explained by referring it, as was earlier suggested, to its major relationships. The dominating concern of the I. W. W. is what Keller calls the maintenance problem. Their philosophy is, in its simple reduction, a stomach philosophy, and their political-industrial revolt could be called without injustice a hunger riot. But there is an important correction to this simple statement. While their way of living has seriously encroached on the urgent minimums of nutrition, shelter, clothing and physical health, it has also long outraged the American labor class traditions touching social life, sex life, self dignity, and ostentation. Had the food and shelter been sufficient, the revolt tendencies might have simmered out, were the migratory labor population not keenly sensitive to traditions of a richer psychological life than mere physical maintenance. Considering their opportunity, the I. W. W. read and discuss abstractions to a surprising extent. In their libraries the few novels are white paged while a translation of Karl Marx or Kautsky, or the dull and theoretical pamphlets of their own leaders, are dog-eared. Few American analysts have realized what firmly held traditions have been established throughout all the working classes by the muckracking literature of the last twenty years. It is rather a hair-raising experience for a conventional member of the middle class to inquire of almost any labor group how they esteem the morals of the commercial middle class. Veblen's acute reasoning touching the decay among industrial labor of the prestige of law and order, of the conventional rights of property and individual liberty seemed to find abundant illustration. A statement that the present industrial order and its control promises a reasonable progress and happiness (and that the middle class are forced to claim) is not only received as a humorous observation by the I. W. W. but today by American Trade Unionism as well.

There will be as many degrees and shades of patriotism as there are social classes in our society. The patriotism which placed fifty thousand volunteers on the rolls of the Officers' Reserve Corps is not an inborn sentiment or anything which arbitrarily came with habitation on American soil. It was an acquired habit of mind and reflected a rich background of social satisfactions, which in the mind of a young officer had sprung from his country, America. Not only the

self-sacrificing quality of this patriotism, but the
very patriotism itself, depends on the existence of
these social satisfactions. Cynical disloyalty and
contempt of the flag must in the light of modern
psychology come from a mind which is devoid of
national gratitude and for whom the United
States stirs no memory of satisfaction or happiness. To those of us who normally feel loyal to the
nation, such a disloyal sentiment brings sharp indignation. As an index of our own sentiment and
our own happy relations to the nation, this indignation has value. As a stimulus to a program or
ethical generalization, it is the cause of vast in-
accuracy and sad injustice. American syndicalism
is not a scheming group dominated by an unconventional and destructive social philosophy. It is
merely a commonplace state of mind. Not such
a mind state as Machiavelli or Robespierre possessed, but a mind stamped by the lowest, most
miserable labor conditions and outlook which
American industrialism produces. To those who
have seen first hand the life of the Western casual
laborer, any reflections on his gratitude or spiritual buoyancy seem ironical humor.

An altogether unwarranted importance has
been given to the syndicalistic philosophy of the

I. W. W. A few leaders use its phraseology. Of these few, not half a dozen know the meaning of French syndicalism or English guild socialism. To the great wandering rank and file, the I. W. W. is simply the only social break in the harsh search for work they have ever had, its headquarters the only competitor of the saloon in which they are welcome. They listen stolidly to their frequent lecturers with an obvious and sustained interest. The lecturer's analysis and dissection of the industrial structures is often as abstract as an economic professor's dissertation on Value. The applause comes when the point is illustrated by some familiar and vigorous action through which the boss is humiliated graphically, told in phrases taken from camp speech. The command of their alleged philosophy is exactly equal to the capacity of a Pittsburgh Republican's to discuss the significance of Schedule K, but the concrete details of industrial renovation find eager interest. The American I. W. W. is a neglected and lonely hobo worker, usually malnourished and in need of medical care. He is as far from a scheming syndicalist, after the French model, as the imagination could conceive. His proven sabotage activities in the West total up a few hop kiln burnings.

Compared to the widespread sabotage in prison industries, where a startlingly large per cent of materials are intentionally ruined, the I. W. W. performance is not worth mentioning. It is to these less romantic economic phases that we must turn for the problem's true cost.

The characteristic of the I. W. W. movement most worthy of serious consideration is the decay of ideals of thrift and industry. To this can be added, in place of the old-time traditional loyalty to the employer, a sustained antagonism to him. The casual laborer of the West drifts off the job without reflection as to the effect of this on the welfare of the employer, feels little interest in the quality of workmanship, and is ever not only a potential striker, but ready to take up political or legal war against the employing class. This sullen hostility has been steadily growing in the last ten years. It is not as melodramatic as sabotage, but vastly more important. To the student it is of major importance because it can be linked up more directly and with more accuracy to its psychological causes. To be short, it is a natural psychic outcome of a distressing and anti-social labor condition. This sullen hostility develops very naturally the surface manifestations of un-patriotism, anti-religion, and unlawful action, but the more important characteristic is the deeper economic one of the growing unreliability and decay of the workmanlike spirit among the migratory laborers.

To revert for a moment to the economic view point. The I. W. W. movement with complete accuracy can be described as the extension of the American labor strike into the zone of casual, migratory labor. All the superficial features, such as its syndicalistic philosophy, its sabotage, threats of burning and destruction, are the natural and normal accompaniments of an organized labor disturbance in this field. The American strike in contrast with the English and German has evolved, for certain psychological reasons, into a militant and violent affair. To the American employer the breaking of a strike satisfies a curious medley of desires. It appeals to his strong and primitive sporting instinct, it is demanded by his highly cultured American individualism, and it satisfies what of legal rights he has imbibed from the loose traditions of *laissez faire*. Taking all the environmental influences which focus on industrial management and property ownership in this country, strike breaking is a very normal managerial activity. Like Calhoun in San Francisco, the American manager has been willing to stake his entire fortune on an anti-union venture, which from no standpoint promised profits or peace. Nowhere else in the world exists the unique American custom of importing strike breakers. The nation-wide anti-union program of the National Manufacturers' Association is even as uniquely American. And these highly individualistic industrial habits are practiced upon a labor class which is in a most peculiar way unfashioned to acquiesce peacefully.

For those who care to see, there is abundant evidence that the Trade Union movement in the United States has become revolutionary. The much advertised split between the American Federation of Labor and the I. W. W. is bridged over with suggestive ease when the prosecution of an I. W. W. case suggests the class struggle. This temper has not prevented the leaders of the American Federation from giving a traditional American patriotism to the present war. But no publicist of note has dared to analyze the spread of embarrassing strikes throughout the United States during the past two months, the most critical months of our war activities. A reasonable induction from the industrial facts would be that the American labor class is not participating in the kind of patriotic fervor that is in vogue among the upper middle class. It is not sufficient to say that their wage demands occupy their attention. Plus this ancient interest is a set of traditional and complicating forces which condition labor's war attitude. The recital of the war profits in steel, in copper, in foods, in medicines, does not fall on ordinary mind receptors. It falls on a labor class mind with a long cultured background of suspicion.

As has already been said, the most vivid chapter in American periodical literature was the period of magazine muckraking. A new and remarkably effective school of pamphleteers arose and operated in a psychologically ripe situation. Their audience had been played on from the early days of the granger movement and was tuned to absorb as truth the bizarre exposé of industrialism. While the magazines a few years ago dropped the propaganda, Federal commissions and state investigations continued and gave dignity and substance to the earlier and more temperamental denunciation. Few members of the middle class know how revolutionary is the material to be found in the Federal Immigration Commission's report, the Federal report on Woman and Child Wage Earners, the Massachusetts Minimum Wage Commission's report, or even the volumes on Occupations of the United States Census. For instance this latter sober source solemnly announces on page seventy-one of its volume on Occupational Statistics that 609,000 of the small boys of the United States between the ages of ten and thirteen are to be accurately cataloged as "workers gainfully employed." The labor class in the United States reads much more on economic matters than the middle class and is more accustomed to meetings and debate in which the material of the reading is used. The middle class is strangely innocent of the publicity dealing with its own activities. Those who teach college economics to the sons and daughters of the middle class are constantly amazed at the contrast between them and the few labor class children who reach the university.

It is not a far cry from the American labor class attitude toward the war to any analysis of the I. W. W. The I. W. W. is, as has been said, the aggressive American labor movement, emerging at the lower and less disciplined social level. The not surprising inability of the American citizen to note the growing class consciousness of the Trade Union movement guaranteed that neither would he make that reasonable prophecy touching the strike methods which would be manifest when this class struggle gained force and form among the migratory casual labor of the West. If the American Trade Union world is only conditionally patriotic in its attitude toward the war, the I. W. W. is violently negative for the same, if more deeply held, reasons. Casualties and deaths in the trenches with its all-diverting suffering at home will reinforce patriotism and silence for a time the class demands and cries, but the ingredients of the social mixture will not be changed in any important degree. War to the American labor world is an episode, and for them the making of a living which dominated their thoughts before the war runs on through the war period itself. So patriotism, in this logic, rests upon the degree of satisfaction and content with which labor views its lot. The labor mind in America is in profound unrest, and it is imperative that those Americans on whom falls the duty of thinking and planning accept such facts as all-determining and do not misuse the moment by useless if admirable moral indignation.

II

The I. W. W. is a union of unskilled workers in large part employed in agriculture and in the production of raw materials. While the I. W. W. appeared in the East at Lawrence, Patterson, and certain other places, at the height of strike activity, its normal habitat is in the upper middle West and the far West from British Columbia down into Old Mexico. But within the past year, apart from the Dakota wheat fields and iron ranges of Minnesota and Michigan, the zone of important activity has been Arizona, California, Washington, Idaho, and Colorado. The present wartime I. W. W. problem is that of its activity in the far West. It is fortunate for analysis that the I. W. W. membership in the West is consistently of one type, and one which has had a uniform economic experience. They are migratory workers currently called hobo labor. The terms "hobo miner," "hobo lumberjack," "the blanket stiff" are familiar and necessary in accurate description of Western labor conditions. Very few of these migratory workers have lived long enough in any one place to establish legal residence and vote, and they are also womanless. Only about ten per cent have been married, and these have either lost their wives or deserted them. Many claim to be "working out," and expect eventually to return to their families. But examination usually discloses the fact that they have not sent money home recently or received letters. They are "floaters" in every social sense. Out of thirty suicides in the cheap lodging houses in San Francisco in the month of December, 1913, but two left behind any word as to their homes or their relatives. Half of the migratories are of American birth, the other half being largely made up of the newer immigration from Southeastern Europe.

The dues-paying membership of the I. W. W. is an uncertain and volatile thing. While a careful study in California in 1915 showed but 4,500 affiliated members of the I. W. W. in that state, it was very evident that the functioning and striking membership was double this or more. In the State of Washington, during the lumber strike of this year, the I. W. W. membership most probably was not over 3,000, but the number of those active in the strike and joining in support of the I. W. W. numbered approximately 7,000. A careful estimate of the membership in the United States gives 75,000. In the history of American labor there has appeared no organization so subject to fluctuation in membership and strength. Several times it seemed on the point of joining the Knights of Labor in the graveyard of labor class movements, but energized by some sudden strike flare it appears again as an active force. This tenacity of life comes because the I. W. W. is not only incapable of legal death, but has in fact no formal politico-legal existence. Its treasury is merely the momentary accumulation of strike funds. Its numerous headquarters are the result of the energy of local secretaries. They are not places for executive direction of the union as much as gregarious centers where the lodging house inhabitant or the hobo with his blanket can find light, a stove, and companionship. In the prohibition states of the West, the I. W. W. hall has been the only social substitute for the saloon to these people. The migratory workers have almost all seen better economic and social days, and carry down into their disorganized labor level traditions, if faint ones, of some degree of dignity and intellectual life. To this group of old time desires the headquarters caters. In times of strike and disorder the headquarters becomes the center of the direct action propaganda. But when this is by, its character changes to the casuals' rest house, and as such is unique in the unskilled workers' history.

It will be of great value to understand the matter of fact conditions under which the American unskilled worker lives and works and is prepared for the drop down into the migratory class.

In 1910, of the 30,091,564 male persons in the United States listed as bread winners, 10,400,000 approximately were in that particular unskilled work from which the migratory is recruited. Under what conditions did this population which furnished the present migratory group work? What was their wage, and how long a period each year were they employed? A typical Chicago slaughter house in 1912 paid 82 per cent of the employees less than 20 cents an hour. This company worked their men on the average of 37½ hours in the week, and this gave the 55 per cent of the men who averaged 17 cents an hour, an income of $6.37 a week. In the steel industry the Government Report of 1910 shows that twenty-nine per cent of the employees worked a seven-day week and twenty per cent a seven-day week with a twelve-hour day. Forty-three per cent worked a twelve-hour day six days a week.

This Federal study reports that 49.69 per cent of the employees received less than 18 cents an hour. This 49.69 per cent is the group of the unskilled. In the steel industry eight per cent of the workers earned less than fourteen cents per hour, and twenty per cent under sixteen cents. The Federal Immigration Commission's report (1910) announced that not one of the twelve basic American industries paid the average head of a family within $100 a year of the minimum for family subsistence, and two-thirds of the twelve industries paid the family head less than $550 a year. Professor Frankfurter's brief before the Supreme Court in the minimum wage case (1916) alleges that half of the wage earners' families in the United States have an income below that needed for adequate subsistence. To quote the authoritative research of Warren and Sydenstricker of the Federal Public Health Service, "in the principal industries, fully one-fourth of the adult male workers who are heads of families earned less than $400, one-half earned less than $600, four-fifths earned less than $800, and less than one-tenth earn as much as $1,000 a year. Approximately one-fourth of the women workers eighteen years of age and over employed in the principal manufacturing industries earned less than $200 a year, and two-thirds less than $400." In reference to the even more vital statistics of total family income these two investigators say, "the conclusion is also indicated that one in every ten or twelve working class families had at the time of the investigation (1912 to 1914) an annual income of less than $300 a year; that nearly a third had incomes of less than $500, and over one-half of the families had incomes of less than $750 a year." The numerous cost of living studies of this period are fairly unanimous that $800 is absolutely necessary for the adequate minimum of subsistence for an American labor class family. Professor Fairchild of Yale said in 1913 "if we fix these standards of living in mind, and then look back over the wage scales given on the foregoing pages, we are struck with the utter inadequacy of the annual incomes of the foreign born to meet even these minimum requirements of decency."

It is reasonable to argue that working class parents suffer in the conventional way in the death of their children. The Federal Children's Bureau reports "for all live babies born in wedlock the infant mortality rate is 130 7/10 in a thousand; it rises to 255 7/10 when the father earns less than $521 a year or less than $10 a week, and falls to eighty-four when he earns $1200 or more."

The irregularity of industrial employment is as important an element as the height of the wage scale. Dr. Devine says that unemployment heads the list of the causes of American destitution. The American coal miner must expect unemployment one-fourth to one-third of his time. In 1908 the unemployment in all trades was 35.7 per cent. Statistics pointed to nearly a twenty per cent loss for all industrial workers in the year through unemployment during this period. The combination of low wages, the unskilled nature of the work and its great irregularity, tends to break the habit and desire for stable industry among the workers. Millions drift into migrating from one industrial center to another in search of work. In these centers nearly all saloon keepers run an employment agency business of a more or less informal kind, and to the saloon the job hunter turns. His fee for the job is to drink up part of his pay check and invariably his history here becomes spotted with a recital of excuses sent to the distant wife instead of money. The worker slides down the scale and out of his industry and joins the millions of unskilled or lost-skilled who float back and forth from Pennsylvania to Missouri and from the lumber camps to the Gulf states and California. They lie up in the winter in the cheap lodging houses, in a state of pseudo-hibernation. Thirty dollars plus a few weeks of ice cutting will weather the winter through. Some 150,000 are in Chicago, as many in New York, 40,000 in San Francisco, even 250 in Phœnix, Arizona. In one San Francisco lodging house, out of 250 beds, there were eight with outside ventilation. A New York study disclosed that the lodging house inmates were eleven times more tubercular than the average population. The beds seldom have linen and the covers are usually dirty quilts which have to be repeatedly fumigated during the winter for vermin. The migratory lies up for the winter with a thirty-dollar stake, according to the report of the Chicago Commission on Unemployment. This often will not stretch over the period, so recourse is had to the street, the saloons, and the city. In a ten-year period, the Chicago police stations gave lodging to 1,275,463 homeless men, and the municipal lodging house to 370,655. Only twenty per cent of these were residents of Chicago.

In the spring this labor group drifts out toward the first work. In main, they beat their way. Between 1901 and 1905 23,964 trespassers were killed on American railroads, and 25,236 injured. These were largely tramps and hoboes. The railroad companies calculated that there were 500,000 hoboes beating their way or waiting at stations to catch on a train, or walking the tracks at any one time. This group might be called the fraction of the migratory millions actually in transit. Numerous statistical studies show that the average period on a job of the migratory is between ten and fourteen days. With a stake of $10 he will retire to a hobo camp beside some stream, his "jungle," as the road vernacular has it, and adding his daily quarter or half a dollar to the "mulligan fund" will live on until the stake is gone. If he tends to live further on the charity of the new comers he is styled a "jungle buzzard" and cast forth. He then resumes his haphazard job-search, the only economic plan in his mind a faint realization that about August he must begin to accumulate his $30 winter stake. Each year finds him physically in worse disrepair, psychologically more hopeless, morally more bitter and anti-social. His importance to any forecast of our nation's future lies in the uncomfortable fact that proportionally he is increasing in number and his recruiting group above is increasing in unrest and economic instability. The menace of this drift has not escaped the critical authorities. John R. Commons, of Wisconsin, in an analysis of the labor unrest in America and the danger of class conflict said, "While immigration continues in great volume, class lines will be forming and reforming, weak and unstable. To prohibit or greatly restrict immigration would bring forth class conflict within a generation." And no less a careful political scientist than Woodrow Wilson wrote in 1913: "Don't you know that some man with eloquent tongue, without conscience, who did not care for the nation, could put this whole country into a flame? Don't you know that this country from one end to the other believes that something is wrong? What an opportunity it would be for some man without conscience to spring up and say 'Follow me!' — and lead in paths of destruction. . . . We are in a temper to reconstruct economic society as we were once in a temper to reconstruct political society."

It is a conventional economic truism that American industrialism is guaranteeing to some

half of the forty millions of our industrial population a life of such limited happiness, of such
restrictions on personal development, and of such
misery and desolation when sickness or accident
comes, that we would be childish political scientists not to see that from such an environment
little sacrificing nation-love, little of ethics, little
of gratitude could come. It is unfortunate that
the scientific findings of our social condition must
use words which sound strangely like the phraseology of the Socialists. But that identity should
be embarrassing logically to the critics of these
findings, not to the scientists. Those who have
investigated and studied in the lower strata of
American labor have long recognized the I. W. W.
as purely a symptom of a certain distressing state
of affairs. The casual migratory laborers are the
finished product of an economic environment
which seems cruelly efficient in turning out
human beings modeled after all the standards
which society abhors. The history of the migratory workers shows that starting with the long
hours and dreary winters of the farms they ran
away from, or the sour-smelling bunk-house in a
coal village, through their character-debasing experience with the drifting "hire and fire" life in

the industries, on to the vicious social and economic life of the winter unemployed, their training predetermined but one outcome, and the environment produced its type. The I. W. W. has importance only as an illustration of a stable American economic process. Its pitiful syndicalism, its street corner opposition to the war, are the inconsequential trimmings. Its strike alone, faithful as it is to the American type, is an illuminating thing. The I. W. W., like the Grangers, the Knights of Labor, the Farmers' Alliance, the Progressive Party, is but a revolt phenomena. The cure lies in the care taking of its psychic antecedents, and the stability of our Republic depends on the degree of courage and science with which we move to the task.

IV

MOTIVES IN ECONOMIC LIFE

THE first quarter of this century is breaking up in a riot of economic irrationalism. The carefully selected efficiency axioms of peaceful life are tossed on the scrap heap, and all society seems to be seeking objects and experiences not found in any of our economists' careful descriptions of the modern industrial order. War allies refuse to unify their military policy, Russia is called on to exhibit a sedate and stable economic life when she lacks wholesale all the attributes to it. And we Americans, despite the notorious record of stringent social accounting imposed by the standards of war efficiency, still lean with fine confidence upon the structure of genial optimism which dominates so much of our national psychology. We look hopefully to see patriotism flow pure and strong from an industrial stratum whose occasional phenomena are Lawrence, McKees Rock, Paterson, Colorado Fuel and Iron, the

Durst hop ranch in California, Everett in Washington, Butte in Montana, Bisbe in Arizona. Though strikes have increased some 300 per cent over peace times, though the American labor world is boiling and sputtering disturbances, bewildering in their variety and rapidity of appearance, our cure is a vague caution to "wait until casualties begin to come," an uneasy contemplation of labor conscription, or a wave of suppression.

Though national unity, economic and military, seems the obvious and essential aim of the patriotic citizen, much done in the name of unification seems to be curiously efficient in producing disunity. The following commonplace incident illustrates this: Note first that Seattle is in a state of extreme industrial unrest. During a single short period this summer, that city had a two weeks' strike paralysis of its street-car system, a threatened walk-out of the gas workers, was the strike center of a complete tie-up of the lumber industry of the state, experienced a building-trades strike involving the entire city, had a walk-out of 30,000 shipbuilders, an express drivers' strike, a candy workers' strike, a newsboys' strike, and enjoyed the beginning of an organization of domestic servants. This city so described becomes the environment for the following incident:

The I. W. W. is strong in the Pacific Northwest, and though it bitterly fights the American Federation of Labor, some of the federation trade unions found in the rough-handed trades, such as lumbering, stevedoring, and even shipbuilding, have drifted toward syndicalism and many of their members even carry secretly the red cards of the I. W. W. The federal government has met the anti-war agitation of the I. W. W. with fair cleverness. When arrests have been made, publicity has been given to the alleged treasonable activity of the leaders, and the government case sustained before the public. The economic activities of the rank and file of the I. W. W., however, have not been interfered with, and their meeting halls in the Northwest continue thronged and the center of their strike activity. *   A Mrs. Sandburg, a Finnish woman, widow, with two children of three and six, lives on a small farm near Seattle. Being destitute she had been awarded a mothers' pension by King County. On November 17 of this year this pension was cut off

---

* It must be remembered that this statement was written in November, 1917.

and the woman recommended for deportation because federal officers asserted that "she was actively working in the interests of the I. W. W., meetings had been held at her home, and members of the organization had visited there frequently." Nothing could be more ingeniously done to focus the interest of a large unrestful labor group in the state of Washington on syndicalism than this incident. This well-intentioned and conventionally patriotic act is not merely inopportune, it is unhappily creative. The great emotional outflow stimulated into existence by the startling announcement of our national danger is being transferred from its desirable nationalistic object and focused on such activities, distressing both socially and economically. It seems an accurate example of the Freudian übertragung, the transference of emotional expression.

It is a far cry from pseudo-political economic problems to a consideration of the delinquencies of modern economics, but there is a vital relation. Our conventional economics today analyzes no phase of industrialism nor the wage relationship, nor citizenship in pecuniary society, in a manner to offer a key to such distressing and complex problems as this. Human nature riots today through our economic structure with ridicule and destruction, and we economists look on helpless and aghast. The menace of the war does not seem potent to quiet revolt or still class cries. The anxiety and apprehension of the economist should not be produced by this cracking of his economic system, but by the poverty of the criticism of industrialism which his science offers. Why are economists mute in the presence of a most obvious crisis in our industrial society? Why have our criticisms of industrialism no sturdy warnings about this unhappy evolution? Why does an agitated officialdom search today in vain among our writings for scientific advice touching labor inefficiency or industrial disloyalty, for prophecies and plans about the rise in our industrialism of economic classes unharmonious and hostile?

The fair answer seems this: We economists speculate little on human motives. We are not curious about the great basis of fact which dynamic and behavioristic psychology has gathered to illustrate the instinct stimulus to human activity. Most of us are not interested to think of what a psychologically full or satisfying life is. We are not curious to know that a great school of behavior analysis called the Freudian has been built around the analysis of the energy outbursts, brought by society's balking of the native human instincts. Our economic literature shows that we are but rarely curious to know whether industrialism is suited to man's inherited nature, or what man in turn will do to our rules of economic conduct in case these rules are repressive. The motives to economic activity which have done the major service in orthodox economic texts and teachings have been either the vague middle-class virtues of thrift, justice, and solvency; or the equally vague moral sentiments of "striving for the welfare of others," "desire for the larger self," "desire to equip oneself well"; or lastly, that labor-saving deduction that man is stimulated in all things economic by his desire to satisfy his wants with the smallest possible effort. All this gentle parody in motive theorizing continued contemporaneously with the output of the rich literature of social and behavioristic psychology which was almost entirely addressed to this very problem of human motives in modern economic society. Noteworthy exceptions are the remarkable series of books by Veblen, the articles and criticisms of Mitchell and Patten, and the

most significant small book by Taussig entitled
Inventors and Money-Makers. It is this complementary field of psychology to which the
economists must turn as these writers have turned
for a vitalization of their basic hypotheses.
There awaits them a bewildering array of studies
of the motives, emotions, and folk ways of our
pecuniary civilization. Generalizations and experiment statistics abound ready-made for any
structure of economic criticism. The human
motives are isolated, described, compared. Business confidence, the release of work energy,
advertising appeal, market vagaries, the basis of
value computations, decay of workmanship, the
labor unrest, decline in the thrift habit, are the
subjects treated. A brief list of these economic-
psychologists is impressive: Veblen, Thorndike,
Hollingworth, Dewey, James, Watson, Holt,
Thomas, Stanley Hall, Jastrow, Patrick, Hob-
house, MacDougall, Hart, Shand, Wallas, Lippmann, Freud, Jung, Prince, Southard, Glueck, Brill,
Bailey, Paton, Cannon, Crile, and so on. One
might say, with fairness, that each one of these
has contributed criticism touching the springs of
human activity of which no economic theorist can
afford to plead ignorance. The stabilizing of the

science of psychology and the vogue among economists of the scientific method will not allow these
psychological findings to be shouldered out by the
careless a priori deductions touching human nature which still dominate our orthodox texts. The
confusion and metaphysical propensities of our
economic theory, our neglect of the consequences
of child labor, our lax interest in national vitality
and health, the unusableness of our theories of
labor unrest and of labor efficiency, our careless
reception of problems of population, eugenics, sex,
and birth control; our crass ignorance of the relation of industry to crime, industry to feeble-mind-
edness, industry to functional insanity, industry
to education; and our astounding indifference to
the field of economic consumption — all this delinquency can be traced back to our refusal to see
that economics was social economics, and that a
full knowledge of man, his instincts, his power of
habit acquisition, his psychological demands and
endurance were an absolute prerequisite to clear
and purposeful thinking on our industrial civilization. MacDougall, the Oxford social psychologist, said in direct point: "Political economy
suffered hardly less from the crude nature of the
psychological assumptions from which it pro-

fessed to deduce the explanations of its facts, and its prescriptions for economic legislation. It would be a libel not altogether devoid of truth to say that the classical political economy was a tissue of false conclusions drawn from false psychological assumptions."

What then are the facts of human nature which the newer psychology offers as the beginning of economic theorizing?

Man is born into his world accompanied by a rich psychical disposition which furnishes him ready-made all his motives for conduct, all his desires, economic or wasteful, moral or depraved, crass or æsthetic. He can show a demand for nothing that is not prompted by this galaxy of instincts. He is a mosaic of unit tendencies to react faithfully in certain ways when certain stimuli are present. As MacDougall has graphically put it, "Take away these instinctive dispositions with their powerful impulses and the human organism would become incapable of activity of any kind; it would lie inert and motionless like a wonderful clockwork whose mainspring had been removed or a steam engine whose fires had been drawn. These impulses are the mental forces which maintain and shape all the life of individuals and societies, and in them we are confronted with the central mystery of life and mind and will."

Thorndike, the Columbia psychologist, in his analysis of human motives, has written, "The behavior of man in the family, in business, in the state, in religion, and in every other affair of life, is rooted in his unlearned original equipment of instincts and capacities. All schemes of improving human life must take account of man's original nature, most of all when their aim is to counteract it."

Veblen wrote in his book, *The Instinct of Workmanship*, "for mankind, as for the other higher animals, the life of the species is conditioned by the complement of instinctive proclivities, and tropismatic aptitudes with which the species is typically endowed. Not only is the continued life of the race dependent upon the adequacy of its instinctive proclivities in this way, but the routine and details of its life are also, in a last resort, determined by these instincts. These are the prime movers in human behavior, as in the behavior of all those animals that show self-direction or discretion. The human activity, in so far as it can be spoken of as conduct, can never exceed the scope of these instinctive dispositions by initiative of which man takes action. Nothing falls within the human scheme of things desirable to be done except what answers to these native proclivities of man. These native proclivities alone make anything worth while, and out of their working emerge not only the purpose and efficiency of life but its substantial pleasures and pains as well."

John Dewey wrote in his *Democracy in Education:* "The instinct activities may be called, metaphorically, spontaneous in the sense that the organs give a strong bias for a certain sort of operation — a bias so strong that we cannot go contrary to it, though by trying to go contrary we may pervert, stunt, and corrupt them."

Cannon, the Harvard physiologist, has said: "More and more it is appearing that in men of all races, and in most of the higher animals, the springs of action are to be found in the influences of certain emotions which express themselves in characteristic instinctive acts."

Instincts to their modern possessor seem unreasoning and unrational, and often embarrassing. To the race, however, they are an efficient and tried guide to conduct, for they are the result of endless experiments of how to fight, to grow, to procreate, under the ruthless valuing mechanism of the competition for survival. These instincts have in the most complete sense of the word, survival value. In fact, outside of some relatively unimportant bodily attributes, the instincts are all that our species in its long evolution has considered worth saving. When one considers the unarmed state in which the soft-bodied human is shoved out in the world to fight for his existence against creatures with thick hides, vise-like jaws, and claws, it becomes clearly evident that if man had not been equipped with an instinctive and unlearned code of efficient competition behavior his struggle on this earth would have been brief and tragic. And also in contrast with his own remote ape ancestors, one could in retrospect see that the survival of the human species must have had as a prerequisite a rich and varied instinct equipment which removed man from the necessity of learning a complete scheme of behavior via the dangerous trial and error method. The species, without some unlearned and protective capacities, would not have lasted the instruction. Within the past ten thousand years nothing in our brilliant experiment with the environment called civilization has been long enough adhered to to bring about a psychical adjustment capable of physical inheritance, and so the basic motives of the business man today remain those of his cave ancestor. The contribution of civilization has been merely an accumulation of more or less useful traditions touching habits accidental in character and questionable in desirability.

All human activity, then, is untiringly actuated by the demand for realization of the instinct wants. If an artificially limited field of human endeavor be called economic life, all of its so-called motives hark directly back to the human instincts for their origin. There are, in truth, no economic motives as such. The motives of economic life are the same as those of the life of art, of vanity and ostentation, of war and crime, of sex. Economic life is merely the life in which instinct gratification is alleged to take on a rational pecuniary habit form. Man is not less a father with a father's parental instinct-interest just because he passes down the street from his home to his office. His business raid into his rival's market has the same naïve charm that tickled the heart of his remote ancestor when in the night he rushed the herds of a near-by clan. A manufacturer tries to tell a conventional world that he resists the closed shop because it is un-American, it loses him money, or is inefficient. A few years ago he was more honest when he said he would run his business as he wished and would allow no man to tell him what to do. His instinct of leadership, reinforced powerfully by his innate instinctive revulsion to the confinement of the closed shop, gave the true stimulus. His opposition is psychological, not ethical.

The importance to me of the description of the innate tendencies or instincts to be here given lies in their relation to my main explanation of economic behavior, which is:

First, that these instinct tendencies are persistent, are far less warped or modified by the environment than we believe; that they function quite as they have for a hundred thousand years; that they, as motives in their various normal or perverted habit form, can at times dominate singly the entire behavior and act as if they were a clear character dominant.

Secondly, that if the environment through any of the conventional instruments of repression, such as extreme religious orthodoxy, economic inferiority, imprisonment, or physical disfigurement, such as short stature or a crippled body, repress the full psychological expression in the field of the instinct tendencies, then a psychic revolt, a slipping into abnormal mental functioning, takes place, with the usual result that society accuses this revolutionist of being either wilfully inefficient, alcoholic, a syndicalist, supersensitive, an agnostic, or insane.

Convention has judged the *normal* man in economic society to be that individual who maintains a certain business placidity, is solvent, safe and not irritating to the delicate structure of credit. Trotter, the English social psychologist, has said that today's current normality has nothing to do with either stability of institutions or human progress. Its single important characteristic is that it is conventional. He urges the imperative need of a new concept of economic normality.

Perhaps one should stop to most seriously emphasize this concept of a new human normality, and also to appreciate the handicap to discussion which comes when every analyzer at a round table has a very different brand of human normality in mind. There is that theoretical 100 per cent normality which is gained for the individual by free mobility plus a full and fine environmental equipment of persons and instruments, and which results in a harmonious and full expression of his psychic potentialities. Since each vigorous life lived under these conditions would generate wisdom in direct proportion to it, I think that an evolutionary and also conventionally desirable progress could be prophesied as a result. This progress has no so-called idealistic goal or direction. It has merely a potentiality for more wisdom, and that wisdom might lead to any of countless possible developments.

A second normality would be that produced by that freedom in instinct expression and that environment which would give far more unconventional experimentation, far more wisdom than we now have, but not the amount which would crack social life by hurrying the change of traditions too much, or destroy those civilization institutions which could be modified with some hope of their higher usefulness. Conscious that man will change, if he is to change, to this latter compromise-normality concept, it is such a normality that I have in mind when I use the term.

In establishing a catalogue of instinct unit characters, one must first meet Thorndike's criticism of such a scheme. He sees the evolution in instinct theorizing toward an acceptance of the theory that there are innumerable special situations and special stimuli each possessed of its particular behavior reflex. All the important new evidence seems to back up this Thorndike contention. However, if the behavior analysis is a less delicate one and laboratory exactness is not demanded, and if merely consistent behavior tendencies are the objects of classification, it seems not unreasonable to build up a working hypothesis in the concrete form of general unit characters of behavior. The innumerable distinct reflex acts described by Thorndike separate out, as he in truth has separated them, into useful groups. These groups can, with great analysis efficiency, be used as unit characters and, properly named, can make up a usable catalogue of man's inherited social tendencies. This the writer has attempted.

The following catalogue of instincts includes those motives to conduct which, under observation, are found to be unlearned, are universal in the species, and which must be used to explain the innumerable similarities in behavior, detached in space and time from each other.

I. *Instinct of gregariousness.* — This innate tendency is exemplified in two ways. Modern economic history is full of that strange irrational phenomenon, "the trek to the city." Even in thinly settled Australia, half the population lives in a few great cities on the coast. In South America and on the Pacific Coast, this same abnormal agglomeration of folk has taken place. The extraordinary piling-up of labor masses in modern London, Berlin, New York, Chicago, has created cities too large for economic efficiency, for recreation or sanitation, and yet, despite their inefficiencies and the food and fire risk, the massing-up continues. Factory employment, though speeded up and paid low wages, grows popular for it caters to gregariousness, and domestic service is shunned for it is a lonely job. Huddle and congestion seem the outstanding characteristics of the modern city.

The second exemplification is seen in man's extreme sensitiveness to the opinion of his group — which is an irrational gregarious reflex. This instinct is the psychic basis for his proclivity to react to mob suggestion and hysteria. In a strike, each striker has a perfectly biological capacity for violence if the group seems to will it. Because of this same gregariousness, a panic can sweep Wall Street, or an anti-pacifist murmur turn into persecution and near-lynching. The crowd members find themselves fatally gripped in the mob drift, they press forward willingly, all yell, and all shake

fists and the most gentle spirited will find himself
pulling at the lynch rope. Royce has said, "Woe
to the society which belittles the power and
menace of the mob mind." The lonely sheep-
herders become in the end irrational, and solitary
confinement ends in insanity or submission.

The slavish following of fashion and fads is
rooted in gregariousness, and the most important
marketing problem is to guess the vagaries of
desire which the mob spirit may select. A great
crowd or festival is satisfying for its own sake.
The installation of a president of a university
needs behind the rows of intellectual delegates a
mass of mere onlooking humanity, and it gets it
by various naïve maneuvers. Crowds seldom disperse as rapidly as they might. They are loath
to destroy their crowdishness, and therefore ir-
rationally hang about. If gregariousness should
weaken, a panic would seize municipal values, and
professional baseball, the advertising business,
and world fairs and conventions would become
impossible.

2. *Instinct of parental bent: motherly behavior: kindliness.* — In terms of sacrifice this is
the most powerful of all instincts. This instinct,
whose main concern is the cherishing of the young

through their helpless period, is strong in women and weak in men. The confident presence in economic life of such anti-child influences as the saloons, licensed prostitution, child labor, the police control of juvenile delinquency, can be well explained by the fact that political control has been an inheritance of the socially indifferent male sex. The coming of women into the franchise promises many interesting and profound economic changes. What little conservation exists today goes back to the male parental instinct for its rather feeble urge.

The disinterested indignation over misery-provoking acts which comes from the parental instinct is the base stimulus to law and order, and furnishes the nebulous but efficient force behind such social vagaries as the Anti-Saloon League, Society for the Prevention of Cruelty to Animals, the Associated Charities, the movement for juvenile courts, prison reform, Belgian relief, the Child Labor League. The competitive egotism of pecuniary society has stifled the habits which express the parental bent. We are not habituated to humanitarianism.

3. *Instinct of curiosity: manipulation: workmanship.* — Curiosity and its attendant desire to

draw near, and if possible to manipulate the curious object, are almost reflex in their simplicity. Of more economic applicability is the innate bent toward workmanship. Veblen has said that man has "a taste for effective work, and a distaste for futile effort." This desire and talent that man has to mould material to fancied ends, be the material clay or the pawns in diplomacy, explains much of human activity, while wages explain little. Prisoners have a horror of prison idleness. Clerks drift out of stereotyped office work, and the monotony of modern industrialism has created a new type of migratory worker. As James has said, "Constructiveness is a genuine and irresistible instinct in man as in the bee or beaver." Man is then not naturally lazy, but innately industrious. Where laziness exists it is an artificial habit, inculcated by civilization. Man has a true quality sense in what he does: there is, then, a "dignity of labor," and it is the job and the industrial environment that produce the slacker, and not the laborer's willful disposition.

4. *Instinct of acquisition: collecting: ownership.* — Man lusts for land, and goes eagerly to the United States, to South America, to Africa for it. It is the real basis of colonial policy and

gives much of the interest to peace parleys. A landless proletariat is an uneasy, thwarted militant proletariat. The cure for unruly Ireland is proven to be peasant proprietorship, and the social menace in the American labor world is the homeless migratory laborer. Russian peasants revolted for land, and this is the single consistent note in the anarchy chaos in Mexico. Man, much of the time, acquires for the mere sake of acquiring. A business man is never rich enough. If, however, making more money uses his acquisitive capacities too little, he may throw this cultivated habit-activity into acquiring Van Dykes or bronzes or Greek antiques, or on a smaller and less æsthetic scale, postage stamps, signatures, or shaving mugs. Asylums are full of pitiful, economic persons who, lost to the laws of social life, continue as automatons to follow an unmodified instinct in picking up and hoarding pins, leaves, scraps of food, paper. The savings banks in large part depend on this inborn tendency for their right to exist.

5. *Instinct of fear and flight.* — Man has the capacity to be fearful under many conditions. His most important fear from an economic standpoint is the stereotyped worker's or business man's

worry over the insecure future. This anxiety or apprehension which is so plentiful up and down the scale of economic life has a profound and distressing influence on the digestive tract, and in turn on the general health. Much of nervous indigestion so common in the ruthless economic competition of today is "fear-indigestion," is instinct reaction, and can only be cured by removing the cause. This removal of the cause is performed many times by an equally instinctive act, flight. Flight in business may take the conventional form of retirement or selling out, but often adopts the unique method of bankruptcy, insanity, or suicide.

6. *Instinct of mental activity: thought.* — To quote Thorndike: "This potent mover [workmanship] of men's economic and recreated activities has its taproot in the instinct of multiform mental and physical activity." To be mentally active, to do something, is instinctively satisfying. Much of invention springs costless from a mind thinking for the sheer joy of it. Organization plans in industry, schemes for market extension, visions of ways to power, all agitate neurones in the brain ready and anxious to give issue in thought. A duty of the environment is not only to allow, but

to encourage, states in which meditation naturally occurs.

7. *The housing or settling instinct.* — In its simplest form, the gunny-sack tents of the tramps, the playhouses of children, the camp in the thicket of the hunter. The squatter has a different feeling for his quarter section when he has a dugout on it. Man innately wants a habitation into which he can retire to sleep or to nurse his wounds, physical or social. The Englishman's home is his castle.

8. *Instinct of migration: homing.* — To every man the coming of spring suggests moving on. The hobo migration begins promptly with the first sunshine, and the tramp instinct fills Europe with questing globe-trotters. The advice, "Go West, young man," was not obeyed on account of the pecuniary gain alone, but because the venture promised satisfaction to the instinct to migrate as well.

9. *Instinct of hunting.* — Man survived in earlier ages through destroying his rivals and killing his game, and these tendencies bit deep into his psychic make-up. Modern man delights in a prize fight or a street brawl, even at times joys in ill news of his own friends, has poorly concealed

pleasure if his competition wrecks a business rival, falls easily into committing atrocities if conventional policing be withdrawn, kills off a trade union, and is an always possible member of a lynching party. He is still a hunter and reverts to his primordial hunt habits with disconcerting zest and expediency. Historic revivals of the hunting urge make an interesting recital of religious inquisitions, witch burnings, college hazings, persecution of suffragettes, of the I. W. W., of the Japanese, or pacifists. All this goes on often under naïve rationalization about justice and patriotism, but it is pure and innate lust to run something down and hurt it.

10. *Instinct of anger: pugnacity.* — In its bodily preparation for action, anger is identical with fear, and fear constitutes the most violent and unreasoning of purposeful dispositions in man. Caught up in anger, all social modifications of conduct tend to become pale, and man functions in primordial attack and defense. Anger and its resulting pugnacity have as their most common excitant the balking or thwarting of another instinct, and this alone explains why man has so jealousy, through all ages, fought for liberty. Pugnacity is the very prerequisite of individual

progress. Employers fight a hampering union, unions a dogmatic employer; every imprisoned man is, in reality, psychically incorrigible; students rebel against an autocratic teacher; street boys gang together to fight a bully; nations are ever ready, yes, hoping, to fight, and their memory of the cost of war is biologically rendered a short one. In fighting, there is a subtle reversion to the primitive standards, and early atrocities become the trench vogue of later months. Patriotism without fighting seems, to western nations, a pallid thing. Most of the vigorous phases of modern civilization remain highly competitive and warlike. Ethics has a long psychological way to go in its vitally necessary task of sublimating the pugnacious bent in man.

11. *Instinct of revolt at confinement: at being limited in liberty of action and choice.* — As above noted, man revolts violently at any oppression, be it of body or soul. Being held physically helpless produces in man and animals such profound functional agitation that death can ensue. Passive resistance can only be possible when nearly all of man's inherited nature is removed. In primitive days, being held was immediately antecedent to being eaten, and the distaste of physical

helplessness is accordingly deep-seated. Belgium would rather resist than live; an I. W. W. would rather go to jail than come meekly off his soap box; the militant suffragettes go through the depravity of forced feeding rather than suffer their inequality; and the worker will starve his family to gain recognition for his union. Man will die for liberty, and droops in prison. So psychically revolting is confinement that the alienists have been forced to create a new disease, a "confinement insanity," a prison psychosis.

12. *Instinct of revulsion.* — The social nausea which society feels towards discussions of sex, venereal disease, leprosy, certain smells, is not founded on willfulness. It is a non-intellectual and innate revulsion to the subject. It is only within the last twenty-five years that the scientific attitude itself has been able to overcome this instinctive repugnance and attack these problems, intimate and perilous to human society, which have languished under the taboo.

13. *Instinct of leadership and mastery.* — It often appears that man seeks leadership and mastery solely because their acquisition places him in a better position to gratify his other instinctive promptings. But there also seems a special grati-

fication in leading and mastery for their own sake. Modern life shows prodigious effort, paid only in the state of being a boss of the gang, a "leading" college man, a "prominent citizen," a secretary or a vice-president, a militia captain or a church elder. A secret ambition to some day lead some group on some quest, be it ethical or economic, is planted deep in our nature. Every dog longs to have his day.

14. *Instinct of subordination: submission.* — In contrast to leadership, man longs at times to follow the fit leader. Soldiers joy in a firm captain, workmen quit a lax though philanthropic employer, instructors thresh under an inefficient though indulgent department head. Eternal independence and its necessary strife are too wearing on the common man and he longs for peace and protection in the shadow of a trust-inspiring leader. To submit under right conditions is not only psychically pleasant, but much of the time to be leaderless is definitely distressing.

15. *Instinct of display: vanity: ostentation.* — This old disposition gives the basic concept for Veblen's remarkable analysis of the economic activities of America's leisure class. The particular state of the industrial arts with its trust control

and divorce of producer and consumer, plus political peace, has taken from man his ancient opportunity to show his unique gifts in ownership of economic goods and in valor. So he is driven in his yearning for attention to perverted activities. He lives to waste conspicuously, wantonly, originally, and, by the refined uselessness of his wasting, to show to the gaping world what an extraordinary person he is. The sensitiveness of social matrons to mention in the society columns, the hysteria to be identified with the changing vagaries of the style, the fear of identification with drab and useful livelihoods, offer in their infinite variety a multitude of important economic phenomena.

16. *Instinct of sex.* — Of the subjects vital to an analysis of life, be they æsthetic or economic, sex has suffered most from the revulsion taboo. Manifestly an instinct which moulds behavior and purposeful planning profoundly, sex as a motive-concept is barred from the economic door. Despite the proven moral and efficiency problems which arise with the postponement of marriage due to modern economic conditions, the massing of unmarried immigrant men into tenement rooms, or the condemning of some millions of mi-

gratory workers to a womanless existence, conventional morality meets every situation by denying the sex instinct, by a blind belief that in some strange way modern economic civilization allows its inmates "to mortify the deeds of the body."

While at any particular moment in our behavior we are a blend or composite of many instinct activities, it is accurate to describe much of behavior as dominated at any one time by either a single instinct or at most two or three. A certain environment can habituate man to a specialization in gratification of a single or a pair of instincts. For instance, war matures and educates habits gratifying the instincts of pugnacity and hunting. At the war front, this habit bent gives basis for gradually sloughing off the humane restrictions governing the fighting, and armies mutually obey their new psychology. Machine-gun men know they will not be taken prisoner and their service is now known as the suicide squad. Hospitals or undefended towns are bombed, a very conventional minimum of attention is fixed for the enemy wounded, the primitive method of warfare of the French African troops which at

first disturbed the ethics of the Allies is now forgotten under the more liberal interpretation under
the revamped war psychology. At home the
citizens of the belligerent countries gain a
cathartic for their overstimulated pugnacious bent
by rioting the People's Council, or tar-and-
feathering the I. W. W., or organizing a man-hunt
for a lately immigrated Austrian or German. It is
quite natural that the actors in these domestic
dramas should build up explanatory rationaliza-
tions for their activity. It is their mild bow to
the fast dimming conventions and traditions of
peace. As a gentle and aged lady deplored, "I
cannot fight, but I can at least go about and listen
and report on the unpatriotic."

The tongue-tied and paralyzed after-dinner
speaker is a single-minded expositor of the strange
instinct of subservience. The worried father of
a sick child seated at his office desk is not an
economic man. His behavior is dominated by
the parental motive, and in this fact is found the
only explanation of his distracted conduct. Veblen
in a shrewd analysis of industrial evolution noted
that the early pre-capitalistic culture, with its
handicraft production and small intimate social
groups, stressed the habits which express the in-

stinct of workmanship and the parental instinct. With the industrial revolution and the immergence into the pecuniary scheme of things of a small property-owning class and a large proletariat, life presented habit opportunities which stressed, in the master class, the so-called egotistical instincts of leadership, hunting, ostentation and vanity, and for the working class removed the opportunities to express the instinct of workmanship and reduced and restricted the other avenues of expression or perverted them to non-evolutionary or anti-social behavior. Instinct perversion rather than freely selected habits of instinct expression seems broadly a just characterization of modern labor-class life. Modern labor unrest has a basis more psychopathological than psychological, and it seems accurate to describe modern industrialism as mentally insanitary.

A remarkable analysis of instinct dominance over behavior is illustrated by the experiments at the Harvard Medical School and described by Professor Cannon. He notes that among the instinct emotions active in man those which are identified with a physical struggle for existence have both a physical and mechanical authority over all other instinct urges to conduct. Like the military general staff, they shoulder aside, in times of stress, the æsthetic and peaceful enthusiasms and mobilize every mental and physical efficiency to their war purpose. The central nervous system is divided by Cannon into three parts, all of which, under peace, function normally. If, however, the brain be stimulated to fear or anger, one of these parts, the so-called "sympathetic part," becomes the dictator. Its particular nerve fibers are, of the three parts, by far the most extensive in their distribution, and permit immediate mobilization of the entire body. Its mobilization consists in "secession of processes in the alimentary canal, thus freeing the energy supplied for other parts, the shifting of blood from the abdominal organs whose activities are deferable to the organs immediately essential to muscular exertion (the lungs, the heart, the central nervous system), the increased vigor of contraction of the heart, the quick abolition of the effects of muscular fatigue, the mobilizing of energy-giving sugar in the circulation — every one of these visceral changes is directly serviceable in making the organism more effective in the violent display of energy which fear or rage or pain may involve."

But the most unique war-footing activity of the body in this vigorous preparedness is the functioning of the adrenal gland. To use Cannon's words: "Adrenin, secreted by the adrenal glands, in time of stress or danger, plays an essential rôle in flooding the blood with sugar, distributes the blood to the heart, lungs, central nervous system and limbs, takes it away from the inhibited organs of the abdomen, it quickly abolishes muscular fatigue and coagulates the blood on injury. These remarkable facts are furthermore associated with some of the most primitive experiences in the life of the higher organisms, experiences common to man and beast — the elemental experiences of pain and fear and rage that come suddenly in critical emergencies."

The conclusion seems both scientific and logical that behavior in anger, fear, pain, and hunger is a basically different behavior from the behavior under repose and economic security. The emotions generated under the conditions of existence-peril seem to make the emotions and motives generative in quiet and peace, pale and unequal. It seems impossible to avoid the conclusion that the most vital part of man's inheritance is one which destines him to continue for some myriads of years ever a fighting animal when certain conditions exist in his environment. Though, through education, man be habituated in social and intelligent behavior, or, through license, in sexual debauchery, still at those times when his life or liberty is threatened, his instinct-emotional nature will inhibit either social thought or sex ideas, and present him as merely an irrational fighting animal.

Since every instinct inherited by man from his tree and cave ancestors, literally sewed into his motivating disposition, has survival value, an environment which balks or thwarts his instinct expression, arouses directly and according to the degree of its menace this unreasoning emotional revolt in him. The chemical proof of this emotional revolt is found by Cannon even in individuals suffering from vague states of worry or anxiety. Here the single problem is the manner in which the angry or fearful person coins his revolt emotion into behavior, and this largely depends upon the right and proper method which society has selected for expressing psychical dissatisfaction. There are folk ways of distress behavior just as certainly as there are of religious enthusiasm or patriotism. Since the emotional tone stimulated by the balking of "minor" instincts would naturally be lower than that intense tone generated by a threatened rending of one's flesh, or imprisonment, to the same degree is the behavior stimulated by the lower-toned emotions less vivid and noteworthy than the blind and frantic resistance to the direct physical threat. The behavior reflex to the emotions generated in a state of worry, anxiety, economic servility, or personal humiliation, instead of expressing itself in violent revolt, is shown in states of mental inertia, loss of interest and power of attention, labor inefficiency, drifting off the job, drink and drugs. These behavior states which under conventional and economic moral theorizing are barrenly and inaccurately described as willful acts, are elemental, irrational, and blind reflex activities. Under conditions which allow the satisfactory expression of man's original inherited proclivities, this warlike specialization of the mind and body is avoided. There the cranial or sacral sections of the peace-footing "automatic" section divide with the warlike "sympathetic" section the authority over the body. Health and nerve reserve are built up, a quiet brain permits rational orderings of the associations of the mind, social behavior habits can influence the order and connections of the neurones and insure their perpetuation; in short, intellectual progress becomes possible.

The instincts and their emotions, coupled with the obedient body, lay down in scientific and exact description the motives which must and will determine human conduct. If a physical environment set itself against the expression of these instinct motives, the human organism is fully and efficiently prepared for a tenacious and destructive revolt against this environment; and if the antagonism persist, the organism is ready to destroy itself and disappear as a species if it fail of a psychical mutation which would make the perverted order endurable.

Even if labor-class children evade those repressive deportment traditions that characterize the life of the middle-class young, at a later date in the life of these working-class members certain powerful forces in their environment, though they work on the less susceptible and less plastic natures of mature individuals, produce obsessions and thwartings which function at times, exclusively almost, in determining the behavior of great classes of the industrial population. The powerful forces of the working-class environment which thwart and balk instinct expression are suggested in the phrases "monotonous work," "dirty work," "simplified work," "mechanized work," the "servile place of labor," "insecure tenure of the job," "hire and fire," "winter unemployment," "the ever found union of the poor district with the crime district," and the "restricated district of prostitution," the "open shop," the "labor turnover," "poverty," the "bread lines," the "scrap heap," "destitution." If we postulate some sixteen instinct unit characters which are present under the laborer's blouse and insistently demand the same gratification that is, with painful care, planned for the college student, in just what kind of perverted compensations must a laborer indulge to make endurable his existence? A western hobo tries in a more or less frenzied way to compensate for a general all-embracing thwarting of his nature by a wonderful concentration of sublimation activities on the wander instinct. The monotony, indignity, dirt, and sexual apologies of, for instance, the unskilled worker's life bring their definite fixations, their definite irrational, inferiority obsessions.

The balked laborer here follows one of the two described lines of conduct: First, he either weak-

ens, becomes inefficient, drifts away, loses interest
in the quality of his work, drinks, deserts his family; or secondly, he indulges in a true type inferiority compensation, and in order to dignify himself,
to eliminate for himself his inferiority in his own
eyes, he strikes or brings on a strike; he commits
violence, or he stays on the job and injures machinery, or mutilates the materials. He is fit food
for dynamite conspiracies. He is ready to make
sabotage a part of his regular habit scheme. His
condition is one of mental stress and unfocused
psychic unrest, and could in all accuracy be called
a definite industrial psychosis. He is neither willful nor responsible, he is suffering from a stereotyped mental disease.

If one leaves the strata of unskilled labor and
investigates the higher economic classes, he finds
parallel conditions. There is a profound unrest
and strong migratory tendency among depart-
ment-store employees. One New York store with
less than three thousand employees has thirteen
thousand pass through its employ in a year. Since
the establishment in American life of big business
with its extensive efficiency systems, its order and
dehumanized discipline, its caste system, as it
were, there has developed among its highly paid

men a persistent unrest, a dissatisfaction and decay of morale which is so noticeable and costly that it has received repeated attention. Even the conventional competitive efficiency of American business is in grave question. I suggest that this unrest is a true revolt psychosis, a definite mental unbalance, an efficiency psychosis, as it were, and has its definite psychic antecedents; and that our present moralizing and guess-solutions are both hopeless and ludicrous.

The dynamic psychology of today describes the present civilization as a repressive environment. For a great number of its inhabitants, a sufficient self-expression is denied. There is for those who care to see, a deep and growing unrest and pessimism. With the increase in knowledge is coming a new realization of the irrational direction of economic evolution. The economists, however, view economic inequality and life degradation as objects, in truth, outside the science. Our value concept is a price mechanism hiding behind a phrase. If we are to play a part in the social readjustment immediately ahead, we must put human nature and human motives into our basic hypotheses. Our value concept must be the yardstick to measure just how fully things and institutions contribute to a full psychological life. We must know more of the meaning of progress. The domination of society by one economic class has for its chief evil the thwarting of the instinct life of the subordinate class and the perversion of the upper class. The extent and characteristics of this evil are only to be estimated when we know the innate potentialities and inherited propensities of man, and the ordering of this knowledge and its application to the changeable economic structure is the task before the trained economists today.

APPENDIX

FOREWORD

THE following report was written about March
1914. Its purpose was to acquaint the Governor with
actual conditions under which migratory and casual
labor lived and worked in California. These conditions described were more or less typical of much of
farm and construction work throughout the state at
that time. It is only fair to state that the ranch referred to in this specific report has since been turned
into a model labor camp. One must read this description of conditions as they were to be able to appreciate the fact that at present, among other revolutionary improvements, there is a reading room for
men, with books, magazines and a victrola. Ford and
Suhr are still in jail, but the California Casual can
hardly recognize today the fly-proof, sanitary haunts
of his unscreened, ungarbaged past. The clean-up of
camps under the State Immigration and Housing Commission has been a concrete accomplished fact. It has
not brought the millennium — for one thing memories
die hard. This report was written before the author
had begun his psychological studies. I imagine at a
later date he would have stressed more vividly the
fact that the proper housing is but one step, though a
vitally important step, toward peaceful industrial relations. Even so, bad housing and camp conditions

loomed too large in California in 1914 to deserve anything less than the spotlight. And a psychologist comes to know, perhaps better than anyone else, that you cannot make over the whole world at once. It is a step forward to clean house.

In editing this report to the Governor certain somewhat unwilling concessions in the form of omissions were made to what we are wont rather approvingly to consider the sensitive feelings of the reading public. In a measure such concessions are justified, yet it was a strongly held theory of the author of this report that it was through just such concessions that society was allowed its continued ignorance in, and thereby cruelly inadequate provisioning for, the physical and psychological wants of the individual. Because of social taboo, human beings must needs continue to find such satisfaction of their normal needs as is possible under conditions which humiliate and degrade.

No point is made in the original report that is not amply substantiated by affidavits. In the main these affidavits have been omitted.

I cannot refrain from calling attention to one phrase in this report which I believe cannot be found in any writings of Carl Parker's after he began his study of psychology. That is the expression on page 189, "he *should* have. . . ." It comes perilously near what he was wont to call "the illogic of blaming." The last function of the psychological economist is to pass moral judgments.

C. S. P.

A REPORT

TO HIS EXCELLENCY HIRAM W. JOHNSON, GOVERNOR OF
CALIFORNIA, BY THE COMMISSION OF IMMIGRATION
AND HOUSING OF CALIFORNIA ON THE CAUSES AND
ALL MATTERS PERTAINING TO THE SO-CALLED
WHEATLAND HOP FIELDS' RIOT AND KILLING OF
AUGUST 3, 1913, AND CONTAINING CERTAIN RECOM-
MENDATION AS A SOLUTION FOR THE PROBLEMS DIS-
CLOSED.

EXCELLENCY:

The occurrence known as the Wheatland Hop Fields' Riot took place on Sunday afternoon, August 3rd, 1913. Growing discontent among the hop pickers over wages, neglected camp sanitation and absence of water in the fields, had resulted in spasmodic meetings of protest on Saturday and Sunday morning, and finally by Sunday noon in a more or less involuntary strike. At five o'clock on Sunday about one thousand pickers gathered about a dance pavilion to listen to speakers. Two automobiles carrying a sheriff's posse drove up to this meeting and officials armed with guns and revolvers attempted to disperse the crowd and to arrest upon a John Doe warrant Richard Ford, the apparent leader of the strike. In the ensuing confusion shooting began and some twenty shots were fired. Two pickers, a deputy sheriff and the district attorney of the county, were killed. The posse fled and the camp remained unpoliced until the state militia arrived at dawn next morning.

The occurrence has grown from a casual, though bloody, event in California labor history into such a focus for discussion and analysis of the state's great migratory labor problem that the incident can well be said to begin, for the commonwealth, a new and momentous labor epoch.

The problem of vagrancy; that of the unemployed and the unemployable; the vexing conflict between the right of agitation and free speech and the law relating to criminal conspiracy; the housing and wages of agricultural laborers; the efficiency and sense of responsibility found in a posse of country deputies; the temper of the country people faced with the confusion and rioting of a labor outbreak; all these problems have found a starting point for their new and vigorous analysis in the Wheatland Riot.

California is yearly becoming more agricultural and less industrial; more seasonal in its demands for labor, more dependent for the harvesting of the yearly crops on the migratory, roofless worker. This new labor status in the State is menacing in its potentiality for spasmodic waves of unrest and sudden, perplexing strikes of unorganized workers. "Passive resistance," the new method in labor warfare, not at all the product of the orthodox labor movement, becomes paralysis because the method, being new, finds no effective legal doctrine or procedure to combat it. The Wheatland affair marks the emergence into strong light of a new and vital problem.

This incident, known as the "Hop-fields' Riot," concerned the hop-pickers employed and camped upon the D—— hop ranch at Wheatland, California, and a Yuba County sheriff's posse which was largely recruited from the county seat, Marysville. There were about 2800 men, women and children camped on the D—— ranch on a low unshaded hill. The camp comprised a motley collection of tents, timber stockades called "bull-pens," gunny sacks stretched over fences, and camp wagons. Toilets were scattered at irregular intervals among these shelters.

A general average taken from 22 affidavits on the subject of the total number of people in the camp gives 2738. This, taken in connection with oral statements made to the investigators by Mr. D—— and D—— Bros.' employees, and a careful inspection of the books of D—— Bros. is the foundation for this estimate of 2800 campers.

The general average of the total number of women and children in the camp, as taken from 19 affidavits, is 1005.

The general average of the total number of aliens or foreigners in the camp, as taken from 18 affidavits, is 1438. It may be noted that during the course of the trial a hop inspector testified that in his gang of 235 he counted 27 different nationalities. One witness testified that he heard speakers using seven different languages at the meeting on Sunday.

Among the important alien groups were Syrian, Mexican, Spanish from the Hawaiian sugar plantations, Japanese, Lithuanian, Italian, Greek, Polish, Hindu, Cuban, Porto Rican, and Swedish. These aliens were unskilled laborers, and many were ignorant of English. They lived in their own native quarters on the grounds, crowded into as few tents or "bull-pens" as was physically possible. They had, as a rule, unclean personal and camp habits, exposed themselves at the pumps in washing, and were indecently careless in the presence of women and children.

The Americans were in the main a casual-working, migratory labor class, with an indifferent standard of life and cleanliness. They were recruited in part from the poor of the country towns, and in part from the impoverished ranches and mining camps of the Sierra foot-hills. A small, but essentially important, fraction were American hoboes. There were many exceptions to these generalizations. Many families were of the better middle class and have been in the habit of using the hop and fruit seasons to get their "country vacations." They were evidently deeply humiliated by their experience, and their indignant condemnation of the filth and sanitary neglect has been, for our investigation, the best standardization of this phase.

Method of the Investigation

This report is founded on a careful personal investigation of the physical facts by all the investigators employed by the commission; upon a close study of the trial of Ford, Suhr, Beck and Bagan at Marysville; upon interviews with witnesses at the trial and with pickers who were present on the ranch during the days before August 3rd and who were not present at the trial, but scattered throughout the State; and upon interviews with residents of Yuba County. The

investigators, in taking testimony, were careful to call
upon the witnesses in their own homes, where amid
familiar surroundings the witnesses could talk easily
and without excitement or prejudice. The testimony
may be classified as follows:

(1) Written statements and affidavits totaling 67.
(2) Of these statements, 52 were made by parties
    who were not called as witnesses at the trial,
    and who were not at any time present in
    Marysville during the course of the trial.
(3) Two of these statements were made by wit-
    nesses called by the prosecution at the trial.
(4) Thirteen of these statements were made by
    witnesses called by the defense at the trial.
    Some of these trial witnesses' statements
    were taken from testimony given under oath
    at the trial.

The large number of defense witnesses is accounted
for by the fact that the defense called many more
witnesses from the people who were laborers on the
hop ranch before the riot; the prosecution's testimony
dealing almost exclusively with the facts of the riot
itself.

(5) Of these written statements, 49 were made by
    men and 18 by women.
(6) In addition to these written statements, there
    were 30 people interviewed at Marysville
    and Wheatland during the investigation,
    whose oral statements corroborate the gen-
    eral conclusion of this report.

There is, therefore, a grand total of 97 witnesses to
the facts contained in this report.

The witnesses who made the written statements have been characterized by the investigators who obtained the statements as follows:

A (1) Perfectly reliable 57
  (2) Doubtful reliability 10
B (1) Keenly observant of conditions..52
  (2) Fairly observant of conditions...15

The proportions of this characterization of those making written statements apply also to the oral statements and interviews.

Wage Conditions

The first important item in the discussion of the labor situation on the ranch is naturally that of wages. In the advertisement for hop-pickers, a copy of which is attached to this report, and which D—— sent broadcast throughout the state, he stated:

"The going price paid for clean picking. A BONUS to all pickers helping us and doing satisfactory work, to the completion of the season — a period of three or four weeks."

This indefinite statement as to the going price seems to have led to no little confusion in the minds of the pickers who were eventually employed.

Ninety cents per 100 pounds was paid by D—— during the first week for hop picking in 1913, to which a so-called "bonus" of 10 cents was added if the picker stayed the three or four weeks' season through. If the pickers quit before the last day of the season, this so-called "bonus" reverted to D——.

If there be a type, or "going" hop-pickers' wage for 1913 in California, it was roughly $1.00 per 100 pounds of hops. There are many affidavits to this effect, and it would certainly seem that this $1.00 per 100 pounds should have been the "going price" on the D—— ranch and the "going price" alluded to in D——'s advertisements, especially when taken in connection with the extra cleanliness required in picking, later discussed herein.

If the "going" wages in that part of the State for hop picking had been paid by D——, and the so-called "bonus" was clearly a reward above this wage for remaining the season through, this system would have been legitimate and blameless, but D—— paid 90 cents per 100 pounds picked when the "going" wage was $1.00, so his alleged "bonus" was in reality a hold-back out of the normal hop picking wage of 1913. He had no more right to the 10 cents than he would have had to 50 cents out of the dollar. There is circumstantial evidence that this alleged bonus was intended at the opening of the season to be, and really acted as, a whip to force pickers to stay out the season in order to receive in the end their normal wage for their weighed and recorded picking. It is suggestive that on the Monday after the Sunday's riot, D—— hastily instituted the wage rate of $1.00 per 100 pounds straight, without the alleged bonus. McCrea, the manager of the D—— ranch, stated to your investigator that wages, in fact, had in past seasons been varied from day to day. If a surplus of pickers came to the grounds and camped during a day, the wage was lowered for the next morning, as the competition of these usually destitute work seekers would insure enough pickers, even at the reduced rate. If the pickers were dissatisfied and drifted out, wages were raised the next morning. If the drift threatened to seriously deplete the force, a "white check," giving a rate of $1.05 for 100 pounds was hastily issued for the next day. This illustrates the use made of the list of variable bonuses noted above. The pressing need of the casual laborers seemed to establish the wage for hop pickers on this ranch, and it is difficult to understand D——'s reference in his advertisements to the "going" or ruling price which was to be paid for picking his hops. On the other hand, D—— found by Friday of the first week that he had about 1000 too many pickers. There is evidence that D—— planned, through State-wide advertising, to bring more pickers to his ranch than he could possibly keep in the field. Some of the pickers state in their affidavits that after they found only occasional opportunities to pick they became disgusted with the work and the increasing filth of the camp and left.

Taking the "bonus" for forfeitures of previous years as a standard, the "bonuses" accruing to D—— through the departure of these discontented workers in 1913 must have been $100 to $150 per day. It will never be settled just how many pickers left before the shooting because of intolerable camp conditions and thus forfeited their "bonus," and how many left because of the shooting and riot. One prior normal year of hop picking showed more than $500 accruing to Durst through forfeited "bonuses" with a pay roll slightly over $19,000.

D——'s hop-drying ovens could not care for the picking of more than 1500 steadily employed pickers, so that one-third of the campers hung around the camp or the office waiting for field tickets. In spite of these facts, it is to be noted that in his advertisements for pickers, D—— stated:

"All white pickers who make application before August 1st will be given work."

It is evident that this broad promise is one that would be well-nigh impossible to fulfill, yet it held out a hope for work to the scattered laborers throughout California, Nevada, and Southern Oregon, and there was no way for them to know whether or not D—— would have sufficient pickers by the time they arrived.

D—— made no effort to reduce the campers in number to correspond to the force needed. The D—— management, knowing exactly what was the sanitary condition of the camp, and aware of the threatened migration of part of the picking force because of it, had in its refusal to correct the abuses, laid itself open to the suspicion of intentional carelessness, because of the gain accruing to D—— in the share of the "bonuses" thus forfeited on account of the pickers leaving.[1]

---

[1] In relation to the above statement as to the surplus number of pickers, the following statement in the affidavit of a hop inspector is noteworthy:

"Adequate facilities for loading and sacking hops were not provided. There were not enough sacks. On one day, after having filled a sack and box by 11 A. M. I was forced to wait until 3 P. M. of the same day, at which time I turned my hops

Oral statements were also made to the investigators to the effect that the pickers were not furnished with enough sacks to keep them busy picking. This situation not only cut down the earning capacity of the pickers but naturally led to dissatisfaction and discontent. There was on this ranch patently no danger of a dearth of labor in this period, even though a part migrated.

D—— has always demanded an unusual standard of cleanliness for his hops, and inspectors have very often forced pickers to go up to the kilns to pick their bags over. We are convinced that the average first picking on this ranch was, in cleanness of hops, up to the average of the district, so that this demand of the inspectors was a material handicap to the pickers. This strict inspection of hops, in connection with the unusual thinness of the hops on the vines, a result of the dry year, accounts in part for the prevailing low average wage of the week's picking prior to the outbreak. The following are typical days' earnings for this period: $1.31, $1.30, $1.11, $.90, $1.80, $1.32, $1.90, $1.25, $.70, $.92, $1.32, $1.82, $1.18, $1.27, $1.41, $1.15. These figures were taken at random from D——'s books.[1]

over to a third party to have weighed, but they were not weighed until 5 P. M. During this time the hops dried in the hot sun and lost weight and I remained idle. I observed this same thing in the case of other persons."

[1] The following extracts from affidavits as to the conditions of picking and the cleanliness required in the hops indicate the difficulties encountered by the pickers, as well as their state of mind:

"I worked for D—— Bros. in 1912, and the requirements for picking hops clean were not as strict as in 1913. They did not allow small stems or leaves in the hops. Many pickers

Sanitary Condition of Camp

In answer to D——'s misleading advertisements
scattered throughout California, Oregon, and even
Nevada, about 3000 people arrived on the ranch
within four days. They came by every conceivable
means of transportation. A great number had no

had to pick their hops over again whenever the inspectors
found that the hops contained a few stems or leaves. The
previous year I worked for D—— Bros. I was able to average
$3.00 a day for the season but in 1913 I just barely made 85
cents a day and worked harder than the previous year."

Following is an extract from the affidavit of an experienced
hop picker:

"I have picked hops in other places and have made as
much as $4.00 a day, but on the D—— ranch I never made
more than 90 cents a day. D—— required the hops to be
picked too clean. He never supplied high-pole men and the
pickers — women and children — had to get poles themselves
and get the hops down. We would also have to pack the hops
about 200 yards to have them weighed and were also compelled to carry them several feet and load them on the wagon.
The hop inspectors would make me and other pickers pick
the hops over again, even if they were clean. The inspectors
would dump the hops out and have us pick them into another
sack. They compelled us to pick little stems and leaves out
of the hops even if not larger than a nickel."

The following last extract from an affidavit on this point
carries great weight, as it was made by a hop inspector on the
ranch:

"The inspection was made so close that the best pickers
could not make over $1.50 a day (when combined with short-
age of sacks, etc.). Because D—— had about 3000 pickers
(he had about 2800 numbers and several worked under one
number) he said he would make an extra clean inspection and
would allow only two hops on one stem, and no leaf bigger
than a nickel, while pickers are usually allowed to strip off
whole handfuls, leaves and all. These conditions were not
stated in his advertisements and no one expected them. All
the pickers were used to making from $2.50 to $5.00 per day
and then, under the above conditions, came down to 85 cents
to $1.50 a day. *Right after August 3rd these standards were
lowered to the usual ones and all sacks needed were furnished.*"

blankets and slept on piles of straw thrown onto the tent floors. These tents were rented from D—— at 75 cents a week, though some old tents were donated by him free of charge. Before these and other accommodations were ready, many slept in the fields. One group of 45 men, women, and children slept packed closely together on a single pile of straw. The moral conditions of these hop-fields are notoriously lax, and this camp was no exception. At least one-half the campers were absolutely destitute, and those who got an opportunity to work were forced to cash in their checks each evening to feed tent companions. There are many recorded instances of actual suffering and hunger.

Perhaps the most vicious sanitary abuse was that of toilets. There were very probably nine of these for the 2800 people. There were certainly not less than 8, nor more than 11. D——'s camp toilet accommodations were one-tenth of the army minimum.

[NOTE. There follow twenty-four affidavits testifying to the consequent unsanitary condition of the camp, and especially its effect on the women and children.]

Garbage

Despite the easily forecasted garbage problem that must of necessity arise in a camp of nearly 3000 people, no real provision was made to take care of the garbage. Food and refuse were thrown out beside and behind the tents and even in the paths. A group of families killed a sheep about Thursday or

Friday of the week of the riot, and on Monday a military surgeon saw the entrails lying beside the tent in the sun as he went there to attend a sick child. This absolute want of garbage disposal without a doubt accounts for a dangerous epidemic of dysentery which had run through the camp by Saturday of that week.

There is ample evidence that the lack of garbage collections was not confined to only one or two localities in camp, but that the refuse was scattered generally over the camp ground.

[Ten affidavits follow describing the condition of the camp due to improper garbage disposal.]

Water

The wells, probably because the water supply had been diminished by two dry years, were absolutely insufficient for the camp. Two of the wells were often pumped dry by sun-up, and the campers were forced either to go to town for water, or to distant wells, or to wells among the ranch buildings. There are numerous affidavits and statements to the effect that two of the wells were out of order or failed to pump water a great deal of the time. . . .

There are numerous statements to the effect that every morning and evening there were lines of from 10 to 35 people at each well waiting to get water. According to the weight of testimony, there were available for the hop pickers on August 3rd, 1913, 5 wells and 2 hydrants.

It is also evident that the condition of the wells was

not what it should have been. The platforms were made of rough board planking and the people were allowed to wash, not only their persons, but their clothes, under the faucets, and on these platforms, allowing the dirty water to drain back into the wells. Moreover, around at least two of the wells small ponds of stagnant water were allowed to form, and garbage and refuse collected in these dump holes and this water drained back into the wells.

The water itself seems to have been the average good valley water, although numerous affidavits state that it had an alkali taste and was often roily and muddy. Moreover, the fact that dirty water was allowed to drain back into the wells signifies that after a few days the supply must necessarily have become more or less contaminated by the disintegrating garbage and vegetable matter.

An important part of the hop field was more than a mile away from the wells, but despite the great heat of this week, ranging from 106 to 110 in the shade, no water was transported to the pickers. D—— told your investigator that although he knew, as a rule, that picking began on the ranch by Thursday or Friday, he never planned to have the water wagon go out to the fields until the following Monday. Upon being asked a reason for this failure to send out a water wagon during these three days of intense heat, Mr. D—— explained that the hop vines were growing in the roadways in the field and would not allow the wagon to enter the field. Confronted with his own statement and also the evidence in numerous affidavits, that a stew wagon and a lemonade wagon

went about the field during these three days selling
their goods to the thirsty pickers, Mr. D—— answered
that the water wagon, in addition to the stew and
lemonade wagons, would have "cluttered up the field
with wagons."

The pickers during this week would be in the fields
by dawn, about 4 o'clock, and about 200 to 300
children were taken into the fields with the women.
By noon, under the burning sun beating down on the
still air held between the rows of vines, the children,
many of whom were very small, were in a pitiable
condition because of the lack of water. Numerous
instances of sickness and partial prostration among
children from five to ten years of age were mentioned
in testimony.[1]

Lemonade and Store Concessions and Ranch Store

D—— had let a lemonade contract to his cousin,
J—— D——, who offered lemonade in the fields at
five cents a glass. This lemonade was proven, upon

---

[1] The few following extracts from affidavits and statements
go further to emphasize the hardships caused by the lack of
drinking water in the fields than any amount of description:
"I carried water to the field in a demijohn and it would
only last about 3 hours and it took an hour to go to camp
for more water."
"We had to carry our own water. A demijohn only lasted
about half a day and we had to walk from a mile to a mile
and a half to refill it. There were a great many children in
the field who cried for water and it was very pitiful to see them
suffer for want of it. Many times I gave my water away to
little children."
"My own boy had to go back nearly two miles to camp
every day at noon and get drinking water and this got hot as
hell and took time from work."

the testimony of the druggist's clerk with whom J——
D—— traded, to have been made largely from citric
acid. . . .

There was also a concession to sell stew and a stew
wagon went out about noon each day among the
pickers. There is a fact in connection with these
lemonade and stew concessions that is tinged with a
certain irony. The lemonade and stew concessions
were entrusted with the duty of furnishing drinking
water to the pickers. It is not strange that all the
witnesses testify that the man who was selling lemonade refused to give away drinking water unless the
thirsty pickers bought lemonade, or that the stew man
gave water only to those who bought stew.[1]

There was absolutely no excuse given for the absence of water in the fields, and the failure of the
ranch management to provide for this suggests, almost
more than any other single incident, the absolute inability of the D—— management to realize any kind

[1] The following is a sample collection of extracts from
the almost pitiful affidavits on this point:

"Water was brought out on the lunch wagon to the field,
but it was free only to those who bought lunches. No other
water was given away."

"J—— D—— sold ice cream cones and lemonade in the
fields and was supposed to give the pickers water for this
privilege. He always had a barrel of water with him on
the wagon and one day we asked him for the water: 'If I give
water away, I will not be albe to sell lemonade or soda.'"

"There was no drinking water furnished to pickers, but there
was a man selling lemonade and ice cream cones. This man
was supposed to furnish drinking water, but refused to give
any away free. He told two boys he would let them have
water at five cents per quart. I purchased a pint of lemonade
Saturday afternoon and I and my children were almost per-
ishing for a drink of water. The lemonade contained a great
deal of citric acid and almost cut the insides out of us."

of social responsibility for the condition of the human beings employed on the ranch.

Store

It is a pertinent fact that D——, while admitting that delivery wagons from Wheatland grocery stores, butcher shops, and bakeries, were strictly forbidden to come on the camp grounds, also admitted that he had a 50 per cent share of the profits of a general food store built by him on the grounds.

Sickness

In due time, and as a natural result of these unsanitary conditions, sickness developed. There is a considerable evidence that dysentery and diarrhoea were prevalent in the camp, and there are also recorded instances not only of malarial fever, but of typhoid. These facts are not surprising considering the fact that the toilets were in such a dilapidated condition; that flies were allowed to breed there, as well as in the horse manure at the barn, by the thousand, and then the uncared for garbage provided an abundant food for these flies so that they became ever-increasing and active carriers of the intestinal infection in the toilets.[1]

Two women, mothers of large families, have written

[1] Following are extracts from affidavits in regard to sickness in the camp:
"I had malarial fever. So did some other women I know."
"I know of one family that all had typhoid."
"I had malarial fever, which lasted until I came to San

in and reported the existence in their families of typhoid, which originated beyond reasonable doubt at the D—— ranch. In one case, it is alleged that four out of a party of five had typhoid. It is a matter of common knowledge that there are at present in every labor camp in California active typhoid carriers and the careless conditions at this camp afforded an excellent opportunity for spreading the disease.

The Employer

R—— D——, the manager and part-owner of the ranch, is an example of a certain type of California employer. The refusal of this type to meet the social responsibilities which come with the hiring of human beings for labor, not only works concrete and cruelly unnecessary misery upon a class little able to combat personal indignity and degradation, but adds fuel to the fire of resentment and unrest which is beginning to burn in the uncared for migratory worker in California. That D—— could refuse his clear duty of trusteeship of a camp on his own ranch which contained hundreds of women and children is a social fact of miserable import. The excuses we have heard of unpreparedness, of alleged ignorance of conditions, are shamed by the proven human suffering and humiliation repeated each day from Wednesday to Sunday of that week. Even where the employer's innate

Francisco, and my friends also had it. Many became ill with malarial fever."

"Two of my children got malarial fever and had to leave on Saturday, August 2nd."

"Every year I worked for D—— there were cases of malaria and typhoid in the camp."

sense of moral obligation fails to point out his duty, he should have realized the insanity of stimulating unrest and bitterness in this inflammable labor force. The riot on the D—— ranch is a California contribution to the literature of the social unrest of America.

The I. W. W.

Of this entire labor force at the D—— ranch, it appears that some 100 had been I. W. W. "card men" or had had affiliations with that organization. There is evidence that there was in this camp a loosely caught together camp local of the I. W. W., with about 30 active members. It is suggestive that these 30 men, through a spasmodic action, and with the aid of the deplorable camp conditions, dominated a heterogeneous mass of 2800 unskilled laborers in 3 days. Some 700 or 800 of the force were of the "hobo" class, in every sense potential I. W. W. strikers. At least 400 knew in a rough way the — for them curiously attractive — philosophy of the I. W. W. and could also sing some of its songs.

Of the 100 odd "card men" of the I. W. W., some had been through the San Diego affair, some had been soap-boxers in Fresno, a dozen had been in the Free Speech fight in Spokane. They sized up the hop field as a ripe opportunity, as the principal defendant, "Blackie" Ford, puts it, "to start something." On Friday, two days after picking started, the practical agitators began working through the camp. Whether or not Ford came to D——'s ranch to foment trouble seems immaterial. There are five Fords in every camp of seasonal laborers in California. We have devoted ourselves in these weeks to such questions as this: "How big a per cent of California's migratory seasonal labor force know the technique of an I. W. W. strike?" "How many of the migratory laborers know when conditions are ripe to 'start something'?" We are convinced that among the individuals of every fruit farm labor group are many potential strikers. Where a group of hoboes sit around a fire under a railroad bridge, many of the group can sing I. W. W. songs without the book. This was not so three years ago. The I. W. W. in California is not a closely organized body with a steady membership. The rank and file know little of the technical organization of industrial life which their written constitution demands. They listen eagerly to the appeal for the "solidarity" of their class. In the dignifying of vagabondage through their crude, but virile, song and verse, in the bitter vilification of the jail turnkey and county sheriff, in their condemnation of the church and its formal social work, they find the vindication of their hobo status which they desire. They cannot sustain a live organization unless they have a strike or free speech fight to stimulate their spirit. It is in their methods of warfare, not in their abstract philosophy or even hatred of law and judges, that danger lies for organized society. Since every one of the 5000 laborers in California who have been at some time connected with the I. W. W. considers himself a "camp delegate" with walking papers to organize a camp local, this small army is watching, as Ford did, for an unsanitary camp or low wage scale, to start the strike which will not only create a new I. W. W. local, but bring fame to the organizer. This common acceptance of direct action and sabotage as the rule of operation, the songs and the common vocabulary are, we feel convinced, the first stirring of a class expression. Class solidarity they have not. That may never come, for the migratory laborer has neither the force nor the vision nor tenacity to hold long enough to the ideal to attain it. But the I. W. W. is teaching a method of action which will give this class expression in violent flare-ups such as that at Wheatland.

The dying away of the organization after the outburst is, therefore, to be expected. Their social condition is a miserable one. Their work, even at the best, must be irregular. They have nothing to lose in a strike and as a leader put it: "A riot and a chance to blackguard a jailer is about the only intellectual fun we have."

Taking into consideration the misery and physical privation and the barren outlook of this life of the seasonal worker, the I. W. W. movement, with all its irresponsible motive and unlawful action, becomes in reality a class protest and the dignity which this characteristic gives it perhaps alone explains the persistence of the organization in the field.

Those attending the protest mass meeting of the Wheatland hop pickers were singing the I. W. W. song "Mr. Block" when the sheriff's posse came up in its automobiles. The crowd had been harangued by an experienced I. W. W. orator — "Blackie" Ford. They had been told, according to evidence, to "knock the blocks off the scissor bills." Ford had taken a sick baby from its mother's arms and, holding it before the eyes of the 1500 people, had cried out: "It's for the life of the kids we're doing this." Not a quarter of the crowd was of a type normally venturesome enough to strike, and yet, when the sheriff went after Ford, he was knocked down and kicked senseless by infuriated men. In the bloody riot which then ensued, District Attorney Manwell, Deputy Sheriff Riordan, a negro Porto Rican and the English boy were shot and killed. Many were wounded. The posse literally fled and the camp remained practically unpoliced until the state militia arrived at dawn the next day.

The question of social responsibility is one of deepest significance. The posse was, I am convinced, over-nervous and, unfortunately, over-rigorous. This can be explained in part by the State-wide apprehension over the I. W. W.; in part by the normal California county posse's attitude toward a labor trouble. A deputy sheriff, at the most critical moment, fired a shot in the air, as he stated: "To sober the crowd." There were armed men in the crowd, for every crowd of 2000 casual laborers includes a score of gunmen. Evidence goes to show that even the gentler mountainfolk in the crowd had been aroused to a sense of personal injury.

D——'s automobile had brought part of the posse. Numberless pickers cling to the belief that the posse was "D——'s police." When Deputy Sheriff Dakin shot into the air, a fusillade took place and when he had fired his last shell an infuriated crowd of men and women chased him to the ranch store, where he was forced to barricade himself. The crowd was dangerous and struck the first blow. The murderous temper which turned the crowd into a mob is incompatible with social existence, let alone social progress. The crowd at the moment of the shooting was a wild and lawless animal. But to your investigator the important subject to analyze is not the guilt or innocence of Ford or Suhr, as the direct stimulators of the mob in action, but to name and standardize the early and equally important contributors to a psychological situation which resulted in an unlawful killing. If this is done, how can we omit either the filth of the hop ranch, the cheap gun talk of the ordinary deputy sheriff, or the unbridled, irresponsible speech of the soap box orator?

Without doubt the propaganda which the I. W. W. had actually adopted for the California seasonal worker can be, in its fairly normal working out in law, a criminal conspiracy, and under that charge, Ford and Suhr have been found guilty of the Wheatland murder. But the important fact is that this propaganda will be carried out, whether unlawful or not. We have talked hours with the I. W. W. leaders and they are absolutely conscious of their position in the eyes of the law. Their only comment is that they are glad if it must be a conspiracy, that it is a criminal conspiracy. They have volunteered the beginning of a cure; it is to clean up the housing and wage problem of the seasonal worker. The shrewdest I. W. W. leader we found said: "We can't agitate in the country unless things are rotten enough to bring the crowd along." They evidently were in Wheatland.

Legal and Economic Aspects

The position taken by the defense and their sympathizers in the course of the trial has not only an economic and social bearing, but many arguments made before the court are distinct efforts to introduce sociological modifications of the law which will have a far-reaching effect on the industrial relations of capital and labor. It is asserted that the common law, on which American jurisprudence is founded, is known as an ever-developing law, which must adapt itself to changing economic and social conditions and, in this connection, it is claimed that the established theories of legal causation must be enlarged to include economic and social factors in the chain of causes leading to a result. Concretely, it is argued:

First, That when unsanitary conditions lead to discontent so intense that the crowd can be incited to bloodshed, those responsible for the unsanitary conditions are to be held legally responsible for the bloodshed as well as the actual inciters of the riot.

Second, That if the law will not reach out so far as to hold the creator of unsanitary, unlivable conditions guilty of bloodshed, at any rate such conditions excuse the inciters from liability, because inciters are the involuntary transmitting agents of an uncontrollable force set in motion by those who created the unlivable conditions.

This involves the problem of how far an inciter or agitator may go without overstepping his "Right of Free Speech." It is contended by the defense in the trial at Marysville that when men are made to work under conditions which normally lead to discontent and revolt, that the words of the agitator are not real factors in producing criminal and bloody results, and that the agitator is to be allowed more latitude and can go further without being legally held responsible than can the agitator who maliciously urges a crowd to violence under normal and ordinary conditions. And this is one of the grounds on which it is urged that the famous "Anarchist's Case" of Spies *v.* The People of Illinois, is to be distinguished from the Wheatland case; that here in Wheatland, the conditions are more vital, overwhelming forces in leading to the riot than were the economic forces in the Spies case, and, therefore, phrases and actions which there were held to go beyond the "Right of Free Speech" would here be within the right, as immaterial and non-contributing causes.

Furthermore, on the legal side, modifications of the law of property are urged. It is argued that modern law no longer holds the rights of private property sacred, that these rights are being constantly regulated and limited, and that in the Wheatland case the owner's traditional rights in relation to his own lands are to be held subject to the right of the laborers to organize thereon. It is urged that a worker on land has a "property right in his job" and that he cannot be made to leave the job, or the land, merely because he is trying to organize his fellow-workers to make a protest as to living and economic conditions. It is urged that the organizing worker cannot be made to leave the job, because the job is *his* property and it is all that he has.

So another curious result of this isolated riot is that the courts are to be brought directly into such controversies, not only to decide technical legal questions, but to consider the cause and effect of economic forces.

Problem

The problem is the great problem of the growing, dangerous friction between the men who hire and those who work, and for the study of which the great Federal Commission on Industrial Relations has been established.

The concrete problem in California is: What must be done to *in fact* remedy the evils of the existing industrial relations between casual, seasonal workers, and their employers, so as to forestall or prevent the insidious, violent work of the agitator who, not interested in improving living conditions and wage conditions, looks upon these only as affording opportunities for stirring up discontent to fan the flames of the "revolution" of his dreams? The seasonal workers are migratory, careless and disorganized, so that there is no effective unit with which the employers can deal or through which the workers can present their demands. Besides, there is ill-will and suspicion and fault on both sides. It is also confidently to be expected that both sides will refuse honestly to take stock of their own deeds and intentions, and condemn the wrong they cannot help but disclose. Therefore, the remedy, of necessity, means the intrusion of a third party.

The Remedy

It is obvious that the violent strike methods adopted by the I. W. W. type agitators, which only incidentally, although effectively, tend to improve camp conditions, are not to be accepted as a solution of the problem. It is also obvious that the conviction of the agitators, such as Ford and Suhr, for murder is not a soluton, but is only the punishment or revenge inflicted by organized society for a past deed. The Remedy lies in prevention.

The laws of the state already provide for the regulation of the sanitation of labor camps, and the Commission of Immigration and Housing has made definite preparations for the enforcement of these laws. The inspectors of this Commission are already at work in the field, and when the camps are opened up at the beginning of the summer season the Commission, acting in conjunction with the State Board of Health, will condemn all dangerously unsanitary camps, and will, if necessary, prosecute the employers to the full extent of the law, which imposes both a heavy fine and imprisonment.

It is the opinion of your investigator that the improvement of living conditions in the labor camps will have the immediate effect of making the recurrence of impassioned, violent strikes and riots not only improbable, but impossible, and furthermore, such improvement will go far towards eradicating the hatred and bitterness in the minds of the employers and in the minds of the roving, migratory laborers. This accomplished, the two conflicting parties will be in a position to meet on a saner, more constructive basis, in solving the further industrial problems arising between them.

As a preliminary to the active enforcement of the labor camp regulation laws, the Commission of Immigration and Housing is preparing to start a statewide campaign of warning and education among the large employers of migratory laborers and among the workers themselves. The employers must be shown that it is essential that living conditions among their employees be improved, not only in fulfillment of their obligations to society in general, but also in order to protect and promote their own welfare and interests. They must come to realize that their own laxity in allowing the existence of unsanitary and filthy conditions gives a much-desired foothold to the very agitators of the revolutionary I. W. W. doctrines whom they so dread. They must learn that unbearable aggravating living conditions inoculate the minds of the otherwise peaceful workers with the germs of bitterness and violence, as was so well exemplified at the Wheatland riot, giving the agitators a fruitful field wherein to sow the seeds of revolt and preach the doctrine of direct action and sabotage.

On the other hand, the migratory laborers must be shown that revolts accompanied by force in scattered and isolated localities not only involve serious breaches of law and lead to crime, but that they accomplish no lasting constructive results in advancing their cause.

The Commission intends to furnish a clearing house

to hear complaints of grievances, of both sides, and act as a mediator or safety valve.

Respectfully submitted,

CARLETON H. PARKER.

Executive Secretary for the State Immigration and Housing Commission of California.

AMERICANA LIBRARY

The City: The Hope of Democracy
By Frederic C. Howe
With a new introduction by Otis A. Pease

Bourbon Democracy of the Middle West, 1865–1896
By Horace Samuel Merrill
With a new introduction by the author

*The Deflation of American Ideals: An Ethical Guide
for New Dealers*
By Edgar Kemler
With a new introduction by Otis L. Graham, Jr.

Borah of Idaho
By Claudius O. Johnson
With a new introduction by the author

The Fight for Conservation
By Gifford Pinchot
With a new introduction by Gerald D. Nash

Upbuilders
By Lincoln Steffens
With a new introduction by Earl Pomeroy

The Progressive Movement
By Benjamin Parke De Witt
With a new introduction by Arthur Mann

*Coxey's Army: A Study of the
Industrial Army Movement of 1894*
By Donald L. McMurry
With a new introduction by John D. Hicks

*Jack London and His Times: An Unconventional
Biography*
By Joan London
With a new introduction by the author

San Francisco's Literary Frontier
By Franklin Walker
With a new introduction by the author

Men of Destiny
By Walter Lippmann
With a new introduction by Richard Lowitt

Woman Suffrage and Politics:
The Inner Story of the Suffrage Movement
By Carrie Chapman Catt and Nettie H. Shuler
With a new introduction by T. A. Larson

The Dry Decade
By Charles Merz
With a new introduction by the author

The Conquest of Arid America
By William E. Smythe
With a new introduction by Lawrence B. Lee

The Territories and the United States, 1861-1890:
Studies in Colonial Administration
By Earl S. Pomeroy
With a new introduction by the author

Why War
By Frederic C. Howe
With a new introduction by W. C. Fowler

Sons of the Wild Jackass
By Ray Tucker and Frederick R. Barkley
With a new introduction by Robert S. Maxwell

My Story
By Tom L. Johnson
With a new introduction by Melvin G. Holli

The Beast
By Ben B. Lindsey and Harvey J. O'Higgins
With a new introduction by Charles E. Larsen

The Liberal Republican Movement
By Earle D. Ross
With a new introduction by John G. Sproat

Growth and Decadence of Constitutional Government
By J. Allen Smith
With a new introduction by Dennis L Thompson

Breaking New Ground
By Gifford Pinchot
With a new introduction by James Penick, Jr.

Spending to Save: The Complete Story of Relief
By Harry L. Hopkins
With a new introduction by Roger Daniels

A Victorian in the Modern World
By Hutchins Hapgood
With a new introduction by Robert Allen Skotheim

The Casual Laborer and Other Essays
By Carleton H. Parker
With a new introduction by Harold M. Hyman